# Non-Adversarial Communication
## *Speaking and Listening from the Heart*

*Arlene Brownell, Ph.D.*
*with*
*Thomas Bache-Wiig*

VELVET
SPRING
PRESS

VELVET SPRING PRESS

Velvet Spring Press
Boulder, CO 80304
303-247-9577
VelvetSpringPress@indra.com

Requests for permission should be addressed to:
Connection Partners, Inc.
P.O. Box 2513
Lyons, CO 80540
www.connectionpartners.com

Brownell, Arlene with Bache-Wiig, Thomas
*Non-Adversarial Communication: Speaking and Listening from the Heart*

Interior Design: J. L. Saloff
Cover Design: Graphic by Manjari
Fonts: Italia Book, Papyrus, Worstveld Sting, Gill Sans, Adobe Jenson,
    Garamond Premier Pro

Library of Congress Control Number: 2007921234
Copyright information available upon request.

10-Digit ISBN: 0-9771232-1-9
13-Digit ISBN: 978-0-9771232-1-6

*Printed on acid-free paper in the United States of America*

This book is dedicated to
every person who yearns for
more inner peace, and for more
peace in the world.

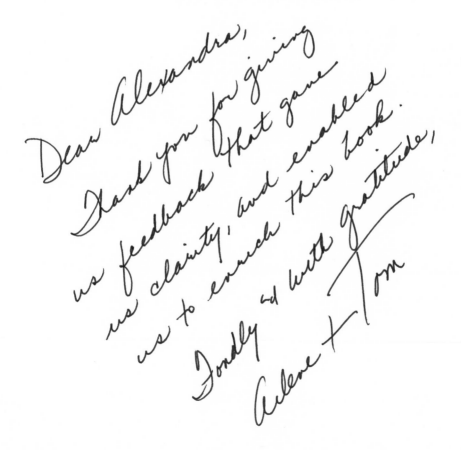

Dear Alexandra,

Thank you for giving
us feedback that gave
us clarity, and enabled
us to enrich this book.

Fondly and with gratitude,

Arlene + Tom

# Table of Contents

# Acknowledgments

This book could not have happened without Tom Bache-Wiig. As colleagues and business partners, we work together to design our NAC trainings, and we regularly confer about how to use NAC to help our clients in our mediations and facilitations, and in our work as collaborative divorce coaches. Much of our understanding of and proficiency with Non-Adversarial Communication (NAC) has come from our continual use of the skills with each other, as wife and husband. As a result, we are both teachers and students for one another. While I have written the words, Tom's contribution is present on each one of the pages of this book.

I thank the hundreds of people we've had the pleasure of training for asking the questions that inspired many of the original practices and activities in this book.

I bless the day I first heard Dr. Marshall Rosenberg talk about his international work using Nonviolent Communication. Both Tom and I have had the good fortune of participating in several trainings with Dr. Rosenberg and with his certified trainers. I consider him a mentor, as do thousands of people around the globe. In addition, I appreciate the contributions to my learning from the teachings of Dr. Robert Gonzales and Dr. Susan Skye. A few of the activities in this book were born from seeds planted by Dr. Rosenberg and his colleagues, including some derived from Lucy Leu's *Nonviolent Communication Companion Workbook*.

Mom, thank you for being willing to reveal our private conversations in order to help others learn.

Several people provided input that enriched and improved upon earlier drafts of this book. My heartfelt thanks to my brother, Albert Neiman, and to Dr. Robert Ashley, Dr. Alexandra Woods, and Christie Coates, MA, JD, for their insightful comments and suggestions.

Thank you to Marj Hahne for her copyediting prowess, and to Jamie Saloff and Manjari Henderson for their artistic abilities. They turned Tom's and my manuscript into a book.

I am forever grateful to John Kadlecek for his guidance that brought this book to fruition. He helped me "to get the book inside of me out, to get it down, and to get it published" just as he said he would.

Arlene Brownell
Lyons, CO
February, 2007

# Preface

*Knowing that words can create happiness or suffering, I am determined to speak truthfully, with words that inspire self-confidence, joy, and hope.*
*—Thich Nhat Hanh*

I first heard Dr. Marshall Rosenberg talk about his work when he was the keynote speaker at a state mediation organizational conference in the fall of 2000. At first, as he told stories to describe a communication process he used in several countries around the world to reduce conflict and heal relationships, I thought he was speaking a foreign language. It wasn't that I couldn't understand what he was saying. I simply had never before experienced language that caressed my eardrums, inviting me to relax, to be more open and receptive.

About fifteen minutes into his talk, he told a story that changed my life. He had been invited to speak at a refugee camp in the Middle East. As he arrived, Marshall was accosted by an enraged man shaking his fist at him and yelling, "Murderer!" Marshall responded by using his particular communication process to understand the man's pain. By the end of the evening, the same man was honoring Marshall with an invitation to come meet his family and break the Ramadan fast together. They walked to the man's home, his arm around Marshall's waist. By the time Marshall finished describing this amazing transformation from rage to affection, I was completely hooked.

Approximately two weeks later, I mediated a conflict between several neighbors. Toward the end of the mediation, after the nine neighbors worked out agreements for resolving several contentious issues, one of them unexpectedly began talking about an incident that had occurred about six weeks before they had begun the mediation process. We all listened in surprise as she described how one evening before going to bed, she had deliberately set her alarm for 4:00 a.m. with the sole purpose of walking downstairs to pound on her living room wall, a wall that adjoined the bedroom of one of the neighbors.

I remembered Dr. Rosenberg's one-hour talk: he'd said that every action anyone takes is an attempt to meet a deep, fundamental human need. I realized that although we were almost finished with the mediation, this woman had an unmet need. I thought about what she had said and then asked her, "Are you describing what you did because you want these neighbors to understand how much their noise was disturbing your sleep, and you were so desperate to be heard that you thought if your noise woke them up, they'd know how you felt?"

The woman's mouth fell open, her face went slack as tension drained away, and she slumped forward with tears in her eyes as she nodded her head in agreement, unable to speak. In that moment, I saw firsthand the power of these communication skills to heal pain and transform distress into relief. I knew then that I was committed to following this path.

# What Is This Book About?

This book is designed to teach you about Non-Adversarial Communication (NAC): its roots deep in your being; its relationship to self-awareness; its skills for articulating your observations, feelings, and needs in a nonthreatening way; and its ability to open opportunities for you to be heard and to deeply hear others, and to ask for what you want in ways that have a better chance of getting you what you need.

# Why Am I Writing This Book?

I began using NAC to help others. Over time, I have found that using these skills has created a profound transformation within me. Now I am able to speak my truth with kindness rather than with anger and defensiveness, and to listen openly for the truths of others without planning my response. The impact I felt when I first heard Dr. Rosenberg talk about his communication process has continued to flourish and grow in my life and in the lives of those I've worked with.

Before I learned NAC, I lived as many of us do: multitasking, plugged into technology, the TV talking at me, never enough time to do everything on my plate. When I began the NAC daily practice of asking myself, "What am I feeling and needing right now?" I discovered that I had no idea. I was completely disconnected from my internal experience, more connected to my computer than to my own life energy. Taking a few minutes each day to disconnect from the outside world in order to connect with my internal experience enabled me to reconnect with myself as a human being.

I began using NAC professionally and personally to create clarity, increase mutual understanding, enhance relationships, and reduce conflict. As I became more proficient in using the skills to listen for what is important to others, and to express my own truth in ways others could hear, I became less angry and more patient. My relationships with my husband, my mother, my brother—and with myself—became less conflictual, more loving and kind. The work with my clients became heartfelt and more effective.

We know the NAC process and skills work, not only from our own experience, but because the people we work with and train tell us that the skills enhance their relationships with family, friends, colleagues, and clients. As more and more people learn to speak and listen in ways that stimulate respectful mutual understanding, the more likely we are to increase harmony in our families, our workplaces, our communities—and in the world.

Writing this book is one way of making a contribution to a groundswell of people who yearn to engage in productive conversation and collaboration. By sharing the NAC tools that changed my life, I hope to help others create more joy and satisfaction in their lives. And ultimately, I wish for this book to be a contribution to creating more peace in the world, one person at a time.

# Who Is This Book For?

This book will help you to:

→ Deepen your relationships with friends and acquaintances.

→ Learn how to identify your own deep yearnings.

→ Engage successfully in challenging conversations or conflicts that you frequently avoid.

→ Express your feelings and needs in ways that can be heard without triggering defensiveness.

→ Remain focused on what's really important instead of being sidetracked by your reactions to what another says or does.

→ Be seen for who you are.

→ Defuse anger and help develop trust and cooperation between people in conflict.

→ Express gratitude in ways that others hear and take in.

→ Be more loving in your language and phrasing.

Because we all are biologically programmed for survival, when our brain's emotion center perceives us to be in immediate danger and we feel threatened (whether or not we really are), we automatically react with fight, flight, or freeze reactions. When our reactions enter our communication, we rarely get the understanding or connection we might have hoped for. In fact, we usually find ourselves deeper in misunderstanding and conflict.

The good news is, with practice we can develop the skills required to transform our own automatic reactions, and those of others, into responses more likely to elicit understanding and connection.

Non-Adversarial Communication (NAC) is not therapy even though its impact is often therapeutic. NAC is based on Dr. Marshall Rosenberg's model as described in his book, *Nonviolent Communication: A Language of Life.*

NAC builds on Dr. Rosenberg's model and process by drawing on relevant information from research in the areas of brain science, emotional intelligence, adult learning, and psychology. We include examples and activities derived from our NAC trainings and from our personal experience, as well as from our professional experience as mediators, facilitators, collaborative divorce coaches, and organizational consultants.

This book offers information and exercises to learn and strengthen skills of Non-Adversarial Communication, develop emotional intelligence, and deepen human connection. The content and exercises in this book are designed for people new to NAC, as well as for people already familiar with the process.

# Use of Terms

In order to write using inclusive, gender-neutral language, I have alternated the use of the pronouns "he" and "she" and "his" and "her" throughout the book.

A few words are used repeatedly throughout the book and deserve some explanation:

**I/we:** Tom and I often work together, and we both contributed conceptually to the content, examples, and activities in this book. Because I was responsible for documenting our thoughts and writing the manuscripts that evolved into this book, the word "I" is used to refer to me, Arlene. When referring to the experience of both authors, the word "we" is used to refer to both of us.

**Intention:** When referring to the specific intention to listen for understanding that is the foundation of Non-Adversarial Communication, the word "intention" is capitalized.

**Trigger/triggered:** "Trigger" refers to an event that stimulates or elicits an automatic, physiological reaction. When we react automatically, we have been "triggered," or stimulated.

**Respond/response:** Use of the word "respond" or its variations is intended to mean that we are making a conscious choice about how we speak or act. Therefore, the terms "respond" and "response" imply accountability and taking responsibility for our words and behaviors.

**React/reaction:** Use of the word "react" or its variations is intended to mean that we are unconsciously reacting to a stimulus. Therefore, "react" and "reaction" are used to convey an automatic, physiological action, words, or behaviors set in motion by what we see, hear, or think.

## Note to Readers

The situations presented as examples in this book that are based on our work with clients have been changed in order to maintain the privacy of the individuals involved.

# Introduction

*It turns out that emotional intelligence is actually the synthesis of both heart and brain functions, weaving together thought and feeling into the marvelously rich fabric of human experience.*
—Hughes, Patterson, and Terrell

## NAC and Emotional Intelligence

When I first heard the woman in the mediation session (see page xvi) describe how she deliberately set her alarm for 4:00 a.m. just to pound on her neighbor's wall, I asked myself, "Why is she telling us this when we are close to wrapping things up?" For a moment, I was totally perplexed. But when I remembered that every action is undertaken to meet a fundamental human need, I found the direction I needed. Later, I came to realize that the skills of Non-Adversarial Communication involve more than brain intelligence and cognitive ability.

Over the past thirty years, neuroscientists studying the brain and the heart have found fascinating evidence supporting the theory that we possess multiple intelligences. One type of intelligence, "emotional intelligence" (EI), is a synthesis of both brain and heart functions.

EI is defined as the ability to identify, express, and manage our own emotional reactions, and to identify and manage the emotional reactions of others. EI is important for making and maintaining mutually satisfying interpersonal relationships and for coping with stress without losing control. In other words, EI is a foundation for achieving both self-management and human connection.

While scientists today debate whether the source of emotional intelligence is in the brain or in the organ of the heart, we use the heart metaphorically to describe the place where feelings and needs reside.

Figure 1 (see next page) illustrates that events or stimuli constantly occur around us as we go about our daily lives. These events stimulate our observations (what we see and hear) *and* our thoughts, whether or not we are fully aware of what we observe and think. In turn, our observations and our thoughts trigger our fundamental human needs. Our needs give rise to our feelings, and those feelings differ depending on whether our needs are met or unmet.

The feelings and needs that come alive are automatic, physiological reactions to our observations and thoughts. When we are unaware of our automatic internal reactions, we remain in automatic reaction, speaking and behaving from our emotional state of the moment. When our needs are unmet and we remain in automatic reaction, we frequently argue, criticize, blame, or judge others or ourselves.

Although we cannot control our automatic reactions (our feelings and needs) to our observations and thoughts, we can choose to develop our EI. When we develop EI, we are able to identify our feelings and needs, and then choose how we want to speak and behave. EI enables us to speak and act with conscious choice rather than automatically react from our emotional state of the moment.

**Figure 1**

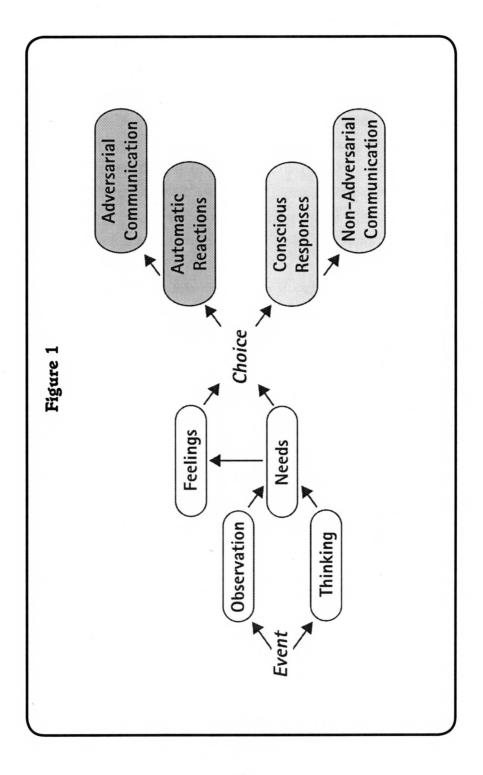

In addition, EI gives us the ability to understand the emotional reactions of others, to respectfully work to help them clarify their feelings and needs, and to help them choose how they wish to speak and behave. I guessed that the woman waking up at 4:00 a.m. to wake up her neighbors felt hopeless because she needed empathy for her distress but didn't know how to communicate her needs in a way that her neighbors would understand. I used EI to decipher the feelings and needs beneath her words.

Learning to discern feelings (the automatic, physiological reactions that occur without our conscious awareness) and the deeper underlying forces (the fundamental human needs) that call forth those reactions is the core of NAC. Using many different tools, NAC enables us to read our own internal reactions and the internal reactions of others. Then we can prevent conflict, build trust, and deepen relationships.

NAC employs two different information-processing systems: emotional intelligence (heart) and brain intelligence (mind). NAC helps us convey the integrated intelligence of our heart and mind through the words we speak and the way we listen. The result is a style of communication that is honest yet kind.

My mother and I butted heads off and on throughout my adolescence and into my adult life, as mothers and daughters often do. NAC finally enabled me to create a different dynamic when, in the middle of a conversation, I recognized that our communication was escalating to an argument I suspected neither of us wanted.

One afternoon during a visit with her, tension rose between us as she refused my offer to help with a problem she was having with her bank. Rather than the grateful acceptance I yearned for, I met with what I told myself was her typical rejection of any help from her "little girl." So I left the room to calm down and gather my thoughts.

When alone, I first allowed myself to silently vent. I complained to myself about how stubborn she is, how she never accepts anything I give her without attempting to give it back, how she refuses all my offers to do anything for her. After a minute or two, I ran out of steam. Once my anger subsided and my blaming stopped, I fully experienced the pain and frustration that my anger toward her had kept at bay. I needed appreciation. I was tired of our clashing and needed ease in our relationship.

Only after discharging my aggravation and experiencing my own feelings (pain and frustration) and needs (appreciation and ease in our relationship) was I able to attempt to guess what she might be feeling and needing. After a few minutes, I returned to the kitchen, where my mother was washing dishes.

"Mom?" I asked, to get her attention. "When you hear me offer to go with you to the bank, do you feel apprehensive because you want recognition for your ability to handle this situation, and you want to be seen as someone still capable of taking care of yourself even though it might take you longer at this age than it did when you were younger?"

As my mother leaned against the sink, all the tension seemed to drain from her body. Her entire posture softened. She looked at me and nodded her head up and down as she said simply, "Yes." In that moment, I realized that my listening beneath my mother's words had shifted the connection between us, and it has been more loving ever since.

## The Fundamentals of NAC

Everyday communication and NAC both consist of two parts: the sending and the receiving of a message expressed in words and accompanied by nonverbal gestures. In our everyday conversations, however, the communication we think we're clearly sending is often heard differently than what we had intended. Sometimes our deeper, more intense feelings seep into and distort our message, even though the words we speak are benign. Sometimes people mistrust our intention and misinterpret what we say. Whatever the reason, a mismatch between the message we think we sent and the message heard can result in defensiveness, hurt feelings, costly mistakes, conflict, damaged relationships, and sometimes violence and death.

It's surprisingly easy to unknowingly inflict pain through our words or through the tone in which we deliver our message. Everyday comments—"Wow, that woman is ugly." "Why can't you be more like your father?" "If you were more disciplined, you'd stick to your diet." "You don't know what you're talking about." "You're always late." "Stop whining." "Can't you do anything right?"—can be a form of verbal abuse that triggers pain, disconnection, and conflict even when we don't intend to do so.

Sometimes we trigger pain and disconnection in our relationships as a function of how we listen. Typically we listen for content and ignore the speaker's underlying internal experience. When listening on the phone, we work on our computers. When we're in meetings, we sort papers and send text messages. While listening, we silently critique what the speaker is saying and think about what we'll say when that person stops talking. When someone seems to talk on endlessly without engaging us, many of us don't know how to redirect the conversation. Instead, we tune out the speaker or interrupt to say what's on our mind.

These disconnecting ways of speaking and listening are so common that we are hardly aware of their dehumanizing impact. Many of us mistakenly believe that the only way to get what we want from others is to use the adversarial forms of speech that we've been exposed to throughout our lives.

Shifting from deeply ingrained habits of criticism, judgment, evaluation, and blame to a gentler, kinder—and honest—style of communication begins with self-awareness and guided work on the basics.

# The Learning Model of This Book: Know, Show, Do

This book follows the "Know, Show, Do" design for adult

learning. The first building block, "Know," involves understanding concepts that are relevant to learning how to speak and listen differently than we do now. Each section, therefore, begins with a brief overview of key concepts.

The next building block for learning, "Show," entails hearing or seeing a demonstration of effective communication skills in order to experience how they differ from the communication styles most of us use. For this reason, each section includes stories and examples to illustrate how NAC differs from the way we normally speak and listen.

Finally, changing behavior requires us to move out of our comfort zone by "Do"-ing things that feel awkward at first. So each section includes exercises and activities designed to awaken awareness, increase sensitivity to internal experience, and develop skills. In addition, the final section of this book, Guide to Daily Practice, contains twelve exercises, each to be undertaken daily for one month. This daily repetition is necessary to create new habits of non-adversarial speaking and listening.

# The Importance of Practice

We once heard a well-respected scientist say that it takes between twenty-one and thirty days of daily use and practice to develop new skills into a habit. If you're looking for a quick fix, be forewarned. Proficiency in Non-Adversarial Communication, as with any other skill, comes not from reading a book but from regular use and practice.

The first time I used NAC to break through the escalating

tension between my mother and me, I went off by myself to silently work through the process before re-engaging with her. I thought about how tired I was of triggering each other in our interactions, and how much I wanted both of our needs to be met in our relationship. I used NAC to connect with my feelings and needs, and to guess what my mom was feeling and needing in our interaction. Then I rehearsed using NAC to express myself in a way she could hear. Because of the history between us, I needed this rehearsal in order to avoid slipping into our customary ways of relating.

The older we are, the more deeply ingrained are our automatic adversarial habits. To move from automatically reacting to consciously choosing how we respond, we must first learn to crawl, and then to walk, before we run a marathon. Further, in order to break habitual patterns and establish new ways of responding, it is important to begin using NAC in situations that either are free of conflict (for example, to express appreciation) or involve only minor conflict before attempting to use the skills in more challenging circumstances. Practicing in relatively easy interactions provides successful experiences and develops skills to use in highly charged, more adversarial situations. The longer the history of conflict in a relationship, the greater the need for rehearsal in order to remain in the NAC process.

Whether we read a book such as this one or go to an NAC training, learning occurs in stages. First we gain intellectual learning about what NAC is, when to use it, and the language and phrasing that make it inviting. With practice, intellectual awareness deepens to body awareness as we experience the internal resonance that occurs when we use NAC to connect with our own fundamental feelings and needs. With continued use and practice, we become more confident in using NAC to help others connect with their fundamental feelings and needs. Finally, as we become more skillful at interrupting our own fight, flight, or freeze reactions by consciously choosing to use NAC to speak and listen non-adversarially, we begin to change on the inside. We become a calmer, less adversarial person.

All the activities in this book have been tested personally by the authors and by willing participants in our trainings and group practice sessions. Our own experience, as well as feedback from our students, convinces us that these practice activities are powerful learning tools.

Designed to create new learning as well as to build on and reinforce previous learning, the practice activities will be helpful to anyone wanting to deepen their skills, introduce NAC to others, or facilitate a practice group—all ways to create a less adversarial world.

# Overview of the Non-Adversarial Communication Process

*Evil... is the absence of empathy.*
*—Captain G. M. Gilbert, psychologist*

## Definition of Non-Adversarial Communication

Non-Adversarial Communication is a process designed to create connection with ourselves and with others. It employs a way of speaking honestly using words and phrasing that invite understanding and connection, as well as a way of listening "beneath" another's words for what is deeply important to that person.

NAC differs from the way we typically communicate because most communication conveys our thoughts, ideas, and judgments about life, but little about our inner experience of life. We rarely converse about our inner experience without evaluating or judging that experience. More specifically, NAC is different because:

→ It involves a specific conscious intention behind every message we express to another.

→ It encourages expression of the simple, observable truth, free of interpretation, evaluation, and judgment.

→ It focuses attention on differentiating thoughts from our feelings and needs.

→ NAC skills help ensure that the message you consciously intend to deliver is the message the listener receives.

→ Using NAC successfully depends upon achieving understanding first, without attachment to a specific strategy or solution.

→ With NAC, one's internal experience is conveyed with kindness rather than with acrimony or unconscious verbal hostility.

# The Components of Non-Adversarial Communication

Non-Adversarial Communication consists of five components: Intention, observation, feelings, needs, and requests. The NAC process helps to establish self-connection and to establish or preserve ongoing relationships among people who need to interact for any purpose, including increasing family harmony, working collaboratively through divorce, cooperating as co-parents after divorce, participating on cross-functional teams at work, interacting within a religious or other organizational community, and creating peaceful dialogue among neighbors.

**Intention:** Intention is the foundation of Non-Adversarial Communication. Intention refers to both an intellectual and an emotional commitment to seek understanding of what is deeply important to everyone involved, and then to direct efforts toward creating solutions that meet at least some of the fundamental human needs of everyone with a stake in the outcome. When we hold on to Intention, then our commitment to understand everyone's needs is a commitment to using the process, even if early attempts feel awkward or progress slowly.

A more complete description of Intention and activities to deepen focus, attention, and Intention are provided in the Intention chapter, which begins on page 31.

**Observation:** An observation consists of what we hear others say (their actual spoken words) or what we see others do (actions that could be captured on video tape). What we observe triggers internal, physiological reactions, some of which are pleasing and some of which are not. We also trigger emotional reactions in each other or within ourselves when we unintentionally confuse our observations with our thoughts—our interpretations, evaluations, criticism, and judgments—and believe that our thoughts are true.

A fuller explanation and activities to build skills to express observations free of evaluation are presented in the Observation chapter (pages 55–79).

**Feelings:** Feelings are internal, physiological reactions to our observations (what we hear or see), as well as to our thoughts. All human beings experience feelings, though trauma or socialization may cause someone to disconnect from conscious awareness of them, or to express a limited range of feelings, such as anger only. Although feelings are a universal human experience, we don't all react to the same event or observation with the same feelings. Reactions we experience as pleasant include feeling happy, loving, intrigued, hopeful, peaceful, and energetic. Reactions we experience as unpleasant include feeling mad, sad, scared, confused, tired, and disconnected.

More detail and activities to build skills to identify and experience our feelings are provided in the Feelings chapter (pages 81–101).

**Needs:** Our needs are our basic, fundamental physical, psychological, and spiritual human desires. Needs are another universal human experience. Many of us understand the basic needs for food, water, and shelter. Few of us have been taught about psychological and spiritual needs for independence, interdependence (including cooperation, fairness, love, nurturing, recognition, respect, support, and trust), play, humor, authenticity, competence, purpose, ease, and harmony.

I think of needs as our life energy. When our needs are met, our spirit is uplifted, and we feel happy, friendly, interested, optimistic, fulfilled, enlivened, etc. When our needs are unmet, we tend to feel diminished in spirit, for example, disgruntled, gloomy, apprehensive, hesitant, weary, or alienated.

A more complete description of needs and activities to develop skills to identify, experience, and meet fundamental human needs are presented in the Needs chapter (pages 103–133).

**Requests:** Requests are the strategies or solutions that we predict will meet the identified needs. There are two types of requests: requests that seek human connection and requests that focus on actions to be taken.

We don't really know if our solution will work until we try it. Most people typically jump to fixing the identified problem without clearly understanding the deeper human needs at play. As a result, most people inadvertently trigger disconnection. Solutions often fail because they don't address what's truly important. When people's needs or interests aren't served by the solutions, they are less invested in keeping their commitments to agreements they've made, and more likely to be disappointed with, or even angered by, the results.

More in-depth information and activities to develop skills to make requests can be found in the Requests chapter (pages 135–162).

# The Process: How It All Works

As illustrated in Figure 1 (see page 5), what we observe (see or hear) and what we think trigger feelings. The specific feeling that we experience is caused by the underlying fundamental human need that is either met or unmet in the situation. The feelings and underlying needs that come alive within us are automatic, physiological reactions that occur without our awareness or conscious control. Once the feelings and needs are aroused, we either react automatically or respond consciously.

When we choose to respond using Non-Adversarial Communication, we first embrace our Intention, clarify our own observation, feelings, and needs, and imagine what the others involved might be feeling and needing. We then decide whether or not to engage with the others involved. If we choose to engage, we decide whether to listen first or to speak first.

When we decide to speak first, we remember our Intention as we express what we observed (what we heard or saw) without mixing in our thoughts about what we observed. Then we express our feelings, and then our needs, as shown in Figure 2. When we listen using NAC, we ground ourselves

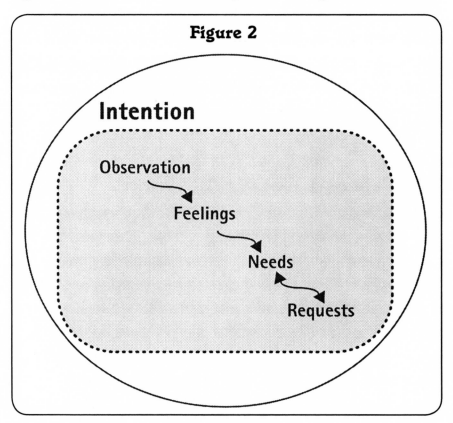

**Figure 2**

Intention

Observation

Feelings

Needs

Requests

in Intention as we focus our attention on understanding the speaker's observation, feelings, and needs. Once everyone's needs are understood, we attend to making requests that we think will resolve the issues while meeting at least some of the needs of everyone involved

To illustrate, let's "listen" to a couple who came to us a few years after they were divorced. We coached them as they used NAC to talk about their financial tensions and the co-parenting of their two children.

**She (forgetting her Intention and speaking adversarially):**

*"I've had a hard time making ends meet, and you haven't been there financially for our children. I've tried to avoid going to court, but I'm tired of struggling to pay bills when you're late with the payments you agreed to make!"*

**He (forgetting his Intention and reacting defensively):**

*"You say that I'm not financially helping to raise our kids, but I've paid you additional money when I've had it, and I've loaned you money when you needed it!"*

**She (remembering her Intention and using NAC with coaching to understand his observation, feelings, and needs):**

*"When you hear me say that you haven't been there financially for our children, are you feeling irritated because you need recognition for the times you've*

*loaned me money or paid a little extra to help me make ends meet?"*

**He (feeling heard):**
*"Yes."*

**He (remembering his Intention and using NAC with coaching to understand her observation, feelings, and needs):**
*"And when you say that you've tried to avoid going back to court, are you frustrated because you'd like some credit for trying to work this out between us even when it's been difficult for you?"*

**She (feeling heard):**
*"Yes."*

**Coach (identifying the needs they expressed, and articulating their unspoken request):**
*"Can you give each other the recognition that you are each asking for?"*

**She:**
*"I want you to know that I do appreciate the times you pitched in extra money when I needed it."*

**He:**
*"Thank you. And I know that you've chosen not to pursue legal action against me, and that you've tried to avoid arguing when I wasn't able to pay you everything I was*

*supposed to. You've helped us to remain calm with each other in front of the kids."*

**She:**
*"Thank you."*

# When Is NAC Useful?

During most conversations, and especially when strong feelings come up, people tend to focus on the content (e.g., who's responsible for taking out the garbage, where the kids are supposed to be at what time, what behavior needs to change before a work promotion will be supported). When we focus on content, we tend to ignore the human reactions to the topics being discussed. Whether we are aware of it or not, however, we all continually react not only to the content or message but also to the specific words and phrasing, the tone of voice, and nonverbal communication, such as posture, gestures, and eye contact.

Throughout a conversation, no matter what the content, we continually move back and forth between reactions of connection and of disconnection. When our needs for connection are met, we are likely to feel relaxed, engaged, receptive, and cooperative. We feel heard and there is a high degree of trust. When our needs for connection are not met, we experience disconnection or separation. We are likely to feel tense, withdrawn, and cautious. As the conversation continues, misunderstanding, mistakes, and conflict are more likely to occur.

When trust is high, our normal styles of communicating may work quite well. However, when we feel out of sync with one another and want to establish or regain connection, Non-Adversarial Communication can create trust and understanding more effectively than our typical ways of speaking and listening.

# The Process In Action: Examples of Speaking and Listening Using NAC

Many people find it challenging to begin using Non-Adversarial Communication, because a style of speaking and listening that incorporates our internal experience is foreign to most of us. Few of us were raised to identify our internal experience or to reveal it without judgment and blame. In addition, it is usually challenging at first to remain in the process while trying to simultaneously hear the content and consciously pay attention to the components of the model (Intention, observation, feelings, needs, and requests). The more tense the interaction, the greater the challenge.

The key to developing NAC skills, as with any skill, is to practice regularly. In addition, when first learning, it is especially important to rehearse both listening and speaking in two or three imagined scenarios prior to engaging with others where there is a high level of conflict. We highly recommend participation in an ongoing practice group where coaching and feedback are provided.

Many people find it easier to initially use the process in a basic and structured way until the skills become more ingrained.

We recommend as a starting point first expressing yourself and listening using the simple but formal structure of the process as shown below.

### Speaking Using NAC

First pause for as long as necessary to marry to Intention (see page 37). Then express yourself using this basic format: "When I see/hear/think about/remember _____, I feel _____ because I need _____. Would you be willing to _____?"

---

### Examples: Speaking

**Typical Way of Speaking:** "When you were away last Wednesday and Thursday, your dog barked and howled all night, and kept me awake both nights. I love dogs but I can't stand this. You've got to figure out a way to keep him quiet or you're going to have to get rid of him."

**Speaking Using NAC with Intention:** "When you were away last Wednesday and Thursday, I was awakened at least five times by a dog I heard barking and howling both nights, and I think it was your dog. I love dogs, but I'm frustrated and exhausted because I need a good night's sleep to think clearly at work. Would you be willing to shut the windows on the side of your house closest to mine before you leave town this week, so we can figure out if that solves the problem?"

---

### Listening Using NAC

First pause for as long as necessary to marry to Intention (see page 37). Then confirm your understanding of what you heard by using this basic format to ask: "When you see/hear/think about/remember _____, do you feel _____ because you need _____?"

---

### Examples: Listening

**Someone says to you:** "When you were away last Wednesday and Thursday, your dog barked and howled all night, and kept me awake both nights. I love dogs but I can't stand this. You've got to figure out a way to keep him quiet or you're going to have to get rid of him."

**Typical Way of Listening:** You say: "I don't know what you're talking about. It must be another dog. I've never heard my dog bark or howl."

**Listening Using NAC with Intention:** You say: "When you remember hearing that dog barking and howling, it sounds like you're really annoyed because you need your sleep, and you'd like to prevent that from happening again, is that accurate?"

---

When listening, it is important that we make a guess (rather than inform, advise, or ask) about what the speaker is feeling and needing, and that we invite correction if our understanding does not match his experience. One reason we offer a guess is to confirm whether or not we are accurately following what the speaker is expressing. Another reason is to help the speaker shift his attention away from his outward thoughts about others, inward toward his own internal experience. A third reason we guess is because the other person is the expert on his own internal experience.

In addition to guessing, we invite correction because the purpose of listening in NAC is not to be right, but to understand. If the speaker provides additional information, she is giving us a gift that enriches our understanding.

When listening, it is useful to slow down the pace of the conversation by creating natural pauses and time for breathing. Slowing down gives the speaker time to actually experience his feelings and needs rather than merely intellectually acknowledge what you guess to be his feelings and needs.

It is also useful to repeat the process by continuing to listen for feelings and needs until the speaker experiences her feelings and needs in her body. It is the experiencing of feelings and needs, rather than the thoughts about what one is feeling and needing, that brings deep clarity. This deeper self-understanding is typically accompanied by a shift to a calmer, quieter state of being.

Once the NAC model becomes ingrained as an internally accessible mental road map, you will find it easier to simultaneously hear the content and listen underneath the content to understand another's observations, feelings, and needs. In addition, you will find it easier to express your own observations, feelings, and needs. Then you will feel more confident that you can use your own style of speaking and listening and still remain in the process.

# Key Learning Points

→ Non-Adversarial Communication is a way of speaking honestly using words and phrasing that invite understanding and connection, as well as a way of listening "beneath" another's words for what is deeply important to that person.

→ NAC differs from the way we typically communicate because, when using NAC, we include information about our experience of life in addition to the other content.

→ Non-Adversarial Communication consists of five components: Intention, observation, feelings, needs, and requests.

→ Intention is the foundation of the NAC process. When we have Intention, we manifest our commitment to seek understanding of what is deeply important to all involved.

→ What we observe (see or hear) triggers feelings. The specific feeling that we experience is caused by the underlying fundamental human need that is either met or unmet in the situation.

→ Once our feelings and needs come alive, we either react automatically or respond consciously.

→ When we decide to speak, we ground ourselves in Intention as we express our observation, our feelings, and our needs. When we listen, we ground ourselves in Intention and focus on understanding the speaker's observation, feelings, and needs.

→ When listening, it is important that we guess (rather than inform, advise, or ask) about what the speaker is feeling and needing.

→ When trust is high, our normal styles of communicating may work quite well. However, when connection needs to be established or reestablished, NAC can more effectively create trust and understanding than our typical ways of speaking and listening.

→ Many people find it challenging to begin using NAC because it focuses on human experience as well as on content. It is essential, as with any skill, to practice and to get coaching and feedback to develop NAC fluency.

# Intention

> *Where the heart is willing*
> *it will find a thousand ways,*
> *but where it is unwilling*
> *it will find a thousand excuses.*
> *—Dayak proverb (Borneo)*

My husband and I recently received an anniversary gift of money from my mother that we applied toward the purchase of a new tree. When we told her that the tree would be our "Mom Tree," she was thrilled. However, she called back the next evening and left a message asking if she had understood correctly that the Mom Tree was a crabapple tree.

In the past, I might have told myself that she was being "overly sensitive" or "focused on image over substance." I probably would have interpreted her question to mean that she was embarrassed to be associated in our minds with a crabapple tree, or I would have assumed that she thought we were hinting that she's crabby. But not this time.

Instead of interpreting or evaluating her question, I listened carefully to her message on our answering machine, and I focused on what she might have been feeling and needing underneath her words. As I heard her say, "Do I understand correctly that the tree is a crabapple tree?" I thought I heard distress or apprehension in her voice. I then guessed that she felt uncomfortable because she needed assurance that selecting a crabapple tree as our "Mom Tree" was meant as a loving gesture, one she could feel proud of.

In fact, Mom had heard correctly; the tree is a crabapple. I wanted our conversation to go as well as possible, so I decided to wait until the next morning before calling her back. I wanted to give myself time to marry to my Intention (see page 37) and to think about how I would answer her question.

In order to connect fully with my Intention, I took two or three deep, long breaths to relax before asking myself what I wanted to happen as a result of returning her call. I knew that I wanted to express myself with loving kindness, and that it was important to me that I first convey my understanding of her need for assurance that calling our tree "Mom Tree" truly is honoring her. I committed to the Intention to use NAC to speak honestly <u>and</u> kindly, and to express myself in a way such that my mother could hear that we will feel loved by her every time we look at our Mom Tree.

When I called her back, I said, "Mom, I heard your question about whether you heard correctly that the Mom Tree is a crabapple tree. This is not just a crabapple tree; it is called a Purple Prince. It will have beautiful purple-pink blossoms in the spring, and turn a spectacular purple-red in the fall. We're planting it in front of our living room window so that we can enjoy its beauty from within the house as well as from the street. We've made it a centerpiece of our home. So I hope you hear that this is not just a crabapple tree."

After my explanation, I knew that my mom had heard me, and that she hung up feeling loved and honored. I had conveyed *my Intention through my words, phrasing, and the tone of my voice.*

~~~~~~~~~~~~~~~~~~~~~~~~~~~~

# What Is Intention and Why Is It Important?

Intention in Non-Adversarial Communication refers to a specific attitude or spirit we bring to our interactions with others. It is the foundation of Non-Adversarial Communication.

Intention refers to both an intellectual and a conscious emotional commitment to see everyone's human needs as equally deserving of respect, to seek understanding of what is deeply important to all involved, and then to direct efforts toward creating solutions that meet at least some of the fundamental human needs of everyone with a stake in the outcome. Intention in NAC is an authentic desire to understand deep human experience without being attached to a specific strategy or solution. This spirit of openness is the essential ingredient for reducing friction, creating harmony, and bringing about reconciliation.

If my intention with my mother had been to simply confirm that she had heard correctly that the tree is a crabapple, I could have called her back, focused on the content of her message, and simply said, "Yes, Mom, it's a crabapple tree. You heard correctly." But I desire to create a loving connection with my mother every chance I get, because I wasn't capable of doing so for many years in the past, and because I realize that one day the opportunity will no longer be available to me. When returning her call, my Intention was to focus on her emotional experience beneath her words.

When we want to win, persuade, convince, fix, force, hurt, manipulate, get even, or do anything other than simply understand what is deeply important to ourselves and to others, we are likely to trigger mistrust, defensiveness, or anger in others. The probable response is an escalation of hostility and forcefulness, which, in turn, triggers an even greater adversarial response.

Many people get what they want by coercing or bullying others, seemingly not knowing or caring that their words and actions damage people and relationships along the way. The higher-functioning part of our brain, the frontal cortex, gives us the capacity to control our responses and to choose to use non-adversarial words and actions. But we also have a lower, animal part of our brain that is predisposed to act defensively. Especially when we are flooded with emotion, our human default reaction is either to act aggressively to get what we want—no matter the damage or the impact on the other person's experience—or to protect ourselves through defensive flight or avoidance.

When flooded with emotion, most people simply react, unconsciously and automatically. When our buttons are pushed, few of us know how to connect with others in a meaningful way, cooperatively resolve different points of view, or get what we want through means that are loving and kind. The first step is to develop the Intention to interact in a way that does no harm

to our self or to another. When entering into a challenging interaction or when wanting to create healthier relationships—with,
for example, friends, family members, coworkers, neighbors,
fellow parishioners, and others—the more important it is to
marry to our Intention.

# Marrying to Intention

When we marry to Intention, we commit to understand and
to respect everyone's needs. This is a long-term commitment
to remain connected to our Intention even if early attempts feel
awkward or progress slowly.

When we hold the Intention to create mutual understanding of what is fundamentally important to all concerned, we
focus our attention on expressing and listening for observations,
feelings, and needs. Once the deep, fundamental needs are
understood, then we can work creatively to formulate requests
(solutions) that we believe will meet the identified needs.

Imagine this interaction between a mother and her four-
year-old daughter:

**Mother (forgetting her Intention to create a more
loving relationship with her daughter, and forgetting to use NAC):**
*"I asked you to pick up your toys and put them in your
toy box. I still see your junk in every nook and cranny of
the living room."*

**Daughter (sitting on the floor, clutching a doll to her chest):**
*"I did pick up. See over there?" (she gestures, pointing to the corner, her lower lip trembling)*

**Mother (feeling irritated and telling herself that her daughter never does what she's asked to do):**
*"You're making me angry. I said pick up your toys right now, or go to your room!"*

**Daughter (yelling):**
*"I did pick up my toys!" (she begins to cry)*

**Mother (observing the situation, remembers her Intention, takes a long, deep breath and uses NAC to restate her observation without the criticism):**
*"Honey, when I see toys on the couch, the chair, and under the coffee table, I feel frustrated because I need order and cleanliness in the space we share. I'm wondering if you were still having fun playing and weren't quite ready to stop, is that right?"*

**Daughter (still crying):**
*"Yeah."*

**Mother:**
*"I guess you're frustrated because you'd like to decide for yourself when to finish putting your toys away?"*

**Daughter (sniffling):**
*"Yeah."*

**Mother (instead of arguing or stating her opinion, continues to guess her daughter's feelings and needs):**
*"And I guess you're hurt because you'd like recognition for the toys you did put away?"*

**Daughter:**
*"Yeah."*

**Mother:**
*"Thank you for putting away the toys you did pick up. How about if we pick up the rest of your toys together and put them in your toy box? Then this room will be clean and you can either go into your room or into the den and keep playing until dinner's ready?"*

**Daughter (stands up):**
*"Okay."*

When our Intention is to create mutual understanding, we manifest it by aligning all our responses to that end. Our choice of words and phrasing, tone of voice, posture, gestures, and how we listen all work together to convey our Intention.

# How Do We Cultivate Intention?

Intention is similar to having a compass to guide us. However, because we are programmed for survival to react defensively, holding on to our Intention is often the most challenging part of using Non-Adversarial Communication. We often encounter resistance and other obstacles, detach from our Intention, and lose our way by reacting unconsciously and automatically. This is especially true when dealing with the people who are closest to us.

When we have a history with people, such as we do with family members, partners, and friends, we are likely to have opinions, images, and beliefs that color how we expect them to be in any given situation. The thoughts we carry about those people get in the way of connecting with our Intention.

Our thoughts (such as the mother telling herself that her daughter never does what she's asked to do) cut off the compassion for others that resides in our heart. Our finger-pointing and the judgments we make about our self or about another create barriers that separate us from our own feelings and needs, and from recognizing that we are all human beings with tender feelings and needs. In order to cultivate Intention, we must first release our images of wrongness and thoughts such as "I'm right, he's wrong," "It's her fault," "If only I hadn't..."

In order to let go of our images of wrongness, it is essential to hear our thoughts and the messages we are telling ourselves. Sometimes we hear the messages and thoughts clearly, but often we are unaware of their presence. Whether we are aware of them or not, judgmental thoughts cut us off from knowing our own and others' internal experience, and from seeing everyone's needs as equally deserving of respect.

One way to disempower the thoughts that prevent us from cultivating Intention is to let them out in private, either by saying them aloud out of the hearing range of others, or by writing them in a journal. For example, visualize an interaction that stimulates your judgmental thoughts, and then express everything that comes to mind until you run out of things to say or write. Then take several deep breaths and repeat this activity for the same interaction until you can't think of anything else to express.

Once your mind quiets down, try answering these questions: "What is my highest Intention for me, for you, and for our relationship?" "What highest good do I really want for me, for you, for us?" Sometimes attempting to answer these questions will set in motion more thoughts about who's right and who's wrong. When that happens, express everything that comes up, as you did before, until your mind quiets down again. Then try answering the questions again.

When we are able to answer the questions with a desire for something good for our self and the other person, such as being able to listen to understand each other, we are reconnecting with the Intention and spirit of NAC. When we are able to reconnect with our Intention, we seek to understand everyone's deep human experience without judgment or criticism and without attachment to a specific outcome.

Once we marry to our Intention, we decide whether we will first listen to the other person, or first express our own observation, feelings, and needs. When we choose to listen to another, we mentally aim the compass of Intention toward that person's heart as a reminder to understand what's deeply and fundamentally important to that person, her feelings, and her needs. When we listen, we focus on understanding the other's observation, feelings, and needs.

When we decide to speak to another, we mentally aim the compass of Intention toward our own heart as a reminder to express what's deeply and fundamentally important in a way that invites the other to hear and understand. Then we express our observation and our internal reaction (our feelings and needs).

For example, when I returned my mom's call, I first stated my observation (that I had heard her question about whether our Mom Tree is a crabapple tree). Then, in everyday language, I confirmed my guess that she needed reassurance (by describing the beauty and place of honor for the tree), and I listened for her reaction so I would know whether or not my description met her need. Finally, I expressed my feeling (hopeful) and my need (to be heard).

The spirit of Non-Adversarial Communication is present only when our Intention is to create mutual understanding and to consider the other's needs as well as our own. When the Intention is missing, the process comes across as mechanical rather than heartfelt. Without Intention, at best we are going through the motions and likely making a bad situation worse.

Drawing on Tibetan and Native American traditions, the meaning of "Intention" comes close to "blessing." When we cultivate Intention as the foundation of a non-adversarial conversation, we can think of the Intention as a blessing for the most good to come from the conversation and to the relationship.

# Key Learning Points

→ Intention is a specific attitude or spirit that is the foundation of Non-Adversarial Communication.

→ Intention refers to both an intellectual and an emotional commitment to seek understanding of what is deeply important to all involved in an interaction, to see everyone's needs as equally deserving of respect, and then to direct efforts toward creating solutions that consider the fundamental human needs of everyone with a stake in the outcome.

→ Because we are programmed for survival to react defensively, holding on to our Intention is often the most challenging part of using Non-Adversarial Communication, especially when dealing with the people who are closest to us.

→ When we are married to Intention, we have a long-term commitment to use the process to understand everyone's needs, even if early attempts feel awkward or progress slowly.

→ In order to cultivate Intention, we must first release our images of wrongness and our judgments, criticism, and blame.

→ When we hold the Intention to create mutual understanding of what is fundamentally important to all concerned, we focus our attention on expressing and listening for observations, feelings, and needs. Once the deep, fundamental needs are understood, then we can work creatively to formulate requests that consider the identified needs of everyone involved.

# Learning Activities to Deepen Intention

## Focusing on Intention and Attention
**Purpose: To strengthen skills of focusing and refocusing**

### What's Needed?

→ 5 uninterrupted minutes

→ A quiet place to sit

### Instructions:

1. Sit quietly with your eyes closed.

2. Breathe deeply through your nose for one minute, silently counting each time you take a breath.

3. As you continue breathing deeply through your nose, commit (intend) to pay attention to feeling the cool air inside the tip of your nose as you breathe in, warm air as your breathe out.

4. When you notice your attention shift from the tip of your nose, gently bring your attention back until you feel the cool air coming in and the warm air going out for six consecutive breaths.

### Suggestions:

→ Repeat this activity for twelve consecutive breaths.

→ Repeat this activity with your eyes open.

→ Repeat this activity in a location where you can hear people talking at a low volume.

**Learning Questions:**

Did you find your mind wandering away from the tip of your nose during this activity?

_____

If your mind wandered, were you able to refocus?

_____

If your mind wandered, were you critical of or gentle with yourself?

_____

# Silent Listening with Intention
**Purpose: To practice listening for understanding**

**What's Needed?**

→ A friend who will talk to you for 4–5 minutes

→ A timer

**Instructions:**

1. Invite a friend to talk to you about an interaction or an event that has some emotional energy.

2. Explain that you are going to listen for a few minutes rather than engage in a dialogue or conversation.

3. Confirm that the other person has a topic in mind.

4. Remind yourself of your Intention to listen solely to understand what is important to the other person.

5. When your Intention is in place, start the timer and listen silently to the other person until the timer goes off.

6. After the timer goes off, ask the other person to describe their experience of being fully listened to.

**Learning Questions:**

Did you find your mind wandering while the other person was speaking?

_____

Did you find yourself wanting to ask questions or offer suggestions?

_____

How did your listening in this activity differ from the way you normally listen?

_____

_____

_____

_____

What did you notice in the other person?

_____

_____

_____

_____

What did you notice in yourself?

_____

_____

_____

How did you manifest your Intention?

_____

_____

_____

What was the impact on the other person?

_____

_____

_____

# Connecting with Intention

**Purpose: To differentiate NAC Intention from other aspirations**

## What's Needed?

→ 10–15 uninterrupted minutes

→ A quiet place to sit

→ A journal or pad of paper

→ A pencil or pen

## Instructions:

1. Sit quietly and breathe deeply for one minute.

2. Think of someone you care about, someone you want in your life for many years to come.

3. Take about five minutes to write your response to this question: "What highest good do I want for me, for you, and for our relationship, now and a few years from now?"

---
 
---
 
---
 
---
 
---
 
---

When you think about what you want as the highest good, do you feel (circle one in each pair): Tense or relaxed? / Receptive or distant? / Curious or mistrustful? / Critical or neutral?

Next, think of an interaction during which you thought the other person wanted to win, persuade, convince, or get even. As you think about that person wanting to win, persuade, convince, or get even, do you feel (circle one in each pair): Tense or relaxed? / Receptive or distant? / Curious or mistrustful? / Critical or neutral?

Next, think of an interaction during which you wanted to win, persuade, convince, or get even. As you think about wanting to win, persuade, convince, or get even, do you feel (circle one in each pair): Tense or relaxed? / Receptive or distant? / Curious or mistrustful? / Critical or neutral?

**Learning Questions:**
What is the difference in your body between feeling tense or feeling relaxed?

_____

_____

_____

_____

Receptive or distant?

_____

_____

_____

Curious or mistrustful?

_____

_____

_____

Critical or neutral?

_____

_____

_____

Which feelings allow you to more deeply understand what is important to another person?

_____

_____

_____

_____

Which feelings invite you to remain engaged with the other person?

_____

_____

_____

≈≈≈≈≈≈≈≈≈≈≈≈≈≈≈≈≈≈≈≈≈≈≈≈

# Observation

The opposite of love is not hate, but judgment.
—Peter Russell

One time when my husband and I arrived at the San Francisco International Airport about one-and-a-half hours before our flight, I estimated there were at least fifty people ahead of me standing in line to check their luggage. As the line slowly meandered toward the check-in counter, I began to worry about whether or not we'd make our flight.

By the time we reached the front of the line, forty-five minutes had passed, and I was sure we would need a lot of luck to catch our flight, even if we were able to rush through check-in and security. However, instead of checking us in, the airline agent on duty waved over from the sidelines a young woman dressed in the airline's regulation navy-blue hat, jacket, and skirt. The agent then turned to us and introduced the young woman in uniform as an agent-in-training who would check us in. With foreboding, I said, "Okay, but we need to hurry to catch our flight."

As the first agent walked away, the agent-in-training logged on to the computer. She looked at the screen, eyes squinting and lips drawn tight as she reached for our tickets, her hand trembling. I stood there thinking, "Just our luck to get someone who doesn't know what she's doing." Ten minutes later, we still were not checked in and I had no idea what was taking so long.

After another minute or so, I could not contain myself. "Can you either hurry up or get help, because you're going to cause us to miss our flight if this takes much longer," I said to the agent-in-training. I noticed that her forehead was glistening with perspiration.

I watched as she squinted at the computer screen. She seemed frozen. I tried to calm myself by thinking that we'd be fine if we missed our flight, that we'd eventually get on a later flight. But after another few minutes, I lost my composure and blurted out, "You're training at our expense. We're going to miss our flight. Get some help now!"

# What Are Observations and Why Are They Important?

An observation refers to what we see or hear, without any interpretation, evaluation, judgment, blame, or other thoughts mixed in. Observations are the simple truth without embellishment.

A pure observation is similar to what a video camera would record. When we play it back, nothing is added to it. We hear and see the same thing each time we view the recording. Because a pure observation is free of thought, an observation is simply information, a word-picture that creates a common frame of reference as the foundation for a conversation.

As shown in Figure 1 (page 5), our thoughts as well as our observations stimulate or trigger an internal, physiological reaction. And like the feelings stimulated by our observations, the feelings stimulated by our thinking differ depending on whether the underlying fundamental need is met or not.

When flooded with feelings, most of us react without clarifying the difference between our observation and our thinking. At the San Francisco Airport, I interpreted the agent-in-training's actions to mean that she didn't know what she was doing. I judged her to be inexperienced and incompetent. Because I thought we were going to miss our flight, I judged that the agent-in-training was processing our check-in too slowly for us to get to the gate on time, and I reacted aggressively, hoping to speed things up. I expressed my thoughts through my critical, judgmental, blaming words, my tone of voice, and my actions.

Now, several years later, after learning NAC, I realize that my own thoughts—first my belief that we'd need luck to catch our flight, and then my judgment of the airline personnel for incompetence—had triggered my anxiety and frustration. Even after we caught our flight, I blamed the agent-in-training for "causing me" such stress, and continued to feel upset because I didn't get the service that "should" have been provided.

# How Does Thinking Differ From Observations?

Our thinking moves us away from the simple truth of our observations (what we see or hear). We inadvertently embellish our observations with our foregone conclusions about how things are. For example, if our boss says she wants to meet with us first thing in the morning, and we interpret that to mean she's going to fire us, we are likely to feel apprehensive and fearful and to approach the meeting defensively in order to protect ourselves from anticipated pain and embarrassment. In the meantime, our boss simply may want to know what we're working on.

We express our thinking in a variety of ways, including:

→ **Comparisons:** "Yours is better or worse, not as good as, smaller, or bigger, than mine."

→ **Criticism and blame:** "It's your fault that I feel this way; if you weren't so cold/stubborn/insensitive, we wouldn't have this problem."

→ **Demands:** "I deserve thanks but you don't even notice how hard I work."

→ **Evaluations and judgments:** "What you said or did is right, wrong, good, bad, helpful, irrelevant."

→ **Interpretations:** "You're angry at me; you don't love me; you're lazy."

Whenever we insert even a hint of judgmental thinking into our observations, no matter how positive the rest of our comments, the other person typically hears only our evaluation, criticism, interpretation, or other judgmental thoughts. She then either withdraws in pain or reacts to us in a defensive or adversarial way.

Our brains function, in large part, to ensure our survival. In addition to taking in what we see, hear or sense, our brains assess whether or not we are in danger. We immediately process that information, too fast for conscious awareness, by automatically interpreting, evaluating, and judging the degree of personal threat to ourselves.

This biological protective device is important but rarely needed in everyday interactions at home, at work, in the community, or when checking in at the airport. Even so, our brains process everything we perceive by filtering the information through our beliefs and expectations.

For example, if someone says, "I hope you don't mind but I'm in a hurry," and moves into line in front of us, if we consider that person to be our enemy, we are likely to interpret his actions and remarks as sarcastic or hostile. However, if we think of that person as our friend, we might interpret the same words and actions as funny.

The problem is that we frequently are unable to differentiate between our observation and our thinking. Until we learn to do so, we will continue to presume that our thoughts are as true as the observation that could be recorded by a video camera.

# What Does an Observation Sound Like?

Unlike interpretation and judgment, pure observation is simply information and is much less likely than interpretation, criticism, or blame to evoke an adversarial response. Pure observation is a context for what we are feeling, needing, and requesting, as shown below.

## Example 1.

### Thinking:

*"You're going to cause us to miss our flight if this takes much longer."*

### Pure Observation:

*"When I see that it's taken forty-five minutes of standing in line to get to this counter, and now eleven more minutes have passed and we're not yet checked in..."*

### A full NAC expression flowing from Intention might continue as:

*"...I feel apprehensive that we're going to miss our flight, and I need reassurance that you're doing everything you can to complete our check-in so we can get to the gate on time. Would you be willing to call the other agent over to help speed up our check-in?"*

## Example 2.

### Thinking:

*"You are the only patient in this ward who never takes a bath. You stink."*

### Pure Observation:

*"When I felt your towel five mornings this week after you'd dressed for the day, it was dry, and I notice an odor of sweat and dirty socks when I stand next to you."*

### A full NAC expression flowing from Intention might continue as:

*"I'm distressed because I want to contribute to your physical well-being but realize that you might need more assistance than I'm able to give to you. I'm wondering if the nurse on duty can determine whether we need some additional resources."*

## Example 3.

### Thinking:

*"Why did you get a grade of C in History? I bet you aren't paying attention in class, and you're watching TV instead of doing your homework."*

### Pure Observation:

*"I see on your report card that you received A's in everything, except for a C in History."*

**A full NAC expression flowing from Intention might continue as:**

*"I'm confused and would like more information about how your studying resulted in the five A's and one C. Would you be willing to sit down now and talk with me for five minutes about how you feel about your grades, and about what we can do to help you raise your grade in History?"*

## Example 4.

### Thinking:

*"Your room is a mess; you're turning into a real slob."*

### Pure Observation:

*"When I see the dish with half-eaten pizza on your desk, your Levis hanging out of your drawer, a shirt on the floor of your closet, three pairs of socks on the floor next to the clothes hamper, a chewed piece of gum on your night-stand, and muddy shoes by the heater..."*

### A full NAC expression flowing from Intention might continue as:

*"...I feel exasperated because I understood you to say that you would have your room cleaned by this morning, before you went to school, and I need for commitments to be honored. I would like to know that I'm communicating clearly, so would you be willing to tell me what you understand me to be saying before we continue further?"*

# The NAC Process

As described earlier, once we marry to our Intention, we decide whether to speak first or to listen first. If we choose to speak first, we state our observation free of thoughts. Then we express how we feel and what we need as a result of what we observed. At this point, we can either request what we believe will meet the need we've identified, or request feedback that lets us know if we've communicated the message as we had hoped. When we hold the Intention to create mutual understanding, our asking if the other person would be willing to say what she understands lets us know whether we used words and phrasing that made it possible for us to be heard in the way we had intended.

When we choose to listen after marrying to Intention, we focus on listening to understand what the speaker saw or heard separate from her thinking, and what she feels and needs in reaction to her observation.

## For example:

### Speaker:

*"I can't believe she cancelled on me again. That's the third time we had plans to do something together and she changed her mind. I think she must have had a better offer. I'm sick of her not keeping her commitments. I've known her since we were in college, and this is a long-standing pattern for her. I should have known better then to offer her the other ticket for the concert. I don't know*

*anyone who can go with me tonight, and I don't want to go by myself."*

**Listener:**

*"When you heard her say that she wasn't going with you to the concert, I'm guessing that you felt furious because you need commitments to be honored. Is that right?"*

**Speaker:**

*"Yes, and she's unwilling to pay for the ticket, so now I'm stuck for the forty bucks. I need that money, and I counted on her to pay me for the ticket."*

**Listener:**

*"So when you heard her say that she wouldn't pay for the ticket, it sounds as if you might be feeling apprehensive about your money situation right now. Is that accurate?"*

As described on page 27, we guess the speaker's feelings and needs (rather than inform, advise, or ask) for several reasons. One reason is that our guessing helps the speaker shift his attention toward his own internal experience, away from his thoughts about others. Guessing also invites the speaker to correct us if he doesn't feel understood.

Once the other person feels heard, we either choose to express ourselves or to ask if the other has a request for how to meet the identified need.

# Key Learning Points

→ In NAC, observations are the simple truth of what we see or hear, free of thoughts, and can be recorded by a video camera.

→ Both our observations and our thinking about what we observe trigger our feelings. Our feelings differ depending on whether our underlying needs are met or unmet.

→ When flooded with feelings, most of us react without differentiating between our observation and our thinking.

→ Expressed judgmental thoughts are likely to trigger defensive, adversarial reactions in others.

→ Our brain processes our observations by automatically evaluating the degree of threat, in order to ensure our survival.

→ Until we learn to separate our observations from our thinking, we tend to believe that our thoughts are true.

→ Once we marry to our Intention, we can choose whether to speak first or to listen first.

→ If we choose to speak first, we begin by stating our observation, and follow with how we feel and what we need as a result of what we observed. Then we can make the request that we believe will meet our need.

→ When we choose to listen first, we focus on listening to understand the speaker's observation free of his thoughts. Then we focus on his feelings and needs that come up in reaction to what he observed.

# Learning Activities to Deepen Skills of Making Pure Observations

Although there are individuals (for example, advanced spiritual beings such as Jesus, Buddha, and Confucius) who respond calmly and non-adversarially when they see or hear something that would carry an intense charge for most of us, we can learn to read our emotional response and to override our automatic fight, flight, or freeze reactions.

Just as airline pilots repeatedly rehearse how they will react if an emergency occurs, we can practice until the response we would like to have available to us is deeply ingrained. Although we may not be able to prevent ourselves from becoming triggered by what we observe, we can develop a habit of pausing and then choosing how to respond in most situations.

The following activities are designed to create awareness of making an observation without evaluation.

# Translating Observation Mixed with Interpretation and Evaluation into Pure Observation

**Purpose: To practice making observations free of evaluation**

## What's Needed?

→ 1–8 people

## Instructions:

This activity can be carried out in pairs, or as friendly competition between two teams of up to four people each.

1. Each person silently selects three objects in the room.

2. The first person chooses one of her selected objects and describes it with as much evaluation and criticism as possible (for example, "the large, ugly oil painting in the muddy-colored frame, hanging too low…"). Then that person calls on another to describe the same object free of evaluation ("The oil painting in the brown wooden frame, approximately 24" x 36", hanging approximately five feet from the ceiling, depicting an ocean with greens and blues…").

3. Continue back and forth until each person has given

two descriptions, one with heavy evaluation and one free of evaluation.

**Learning Questions:**

Which was more challenging for you: describing an object using evaluative language or using language free of evaluation?

_____

Were some evaluative words more difficult to translate into a description free of evaluation? If so, list those words here:

_____

_____

_____

_____

_____

**Suggestions:**

Use your list of words to brainstorm non-evaluative ways to be descriptive with at least one other person who did the activity with you.

Identify one situation in your life where you want to use pure observation in order to minimize conflict and avoid misunderstanding.

_____

_____

_____

_____

_____

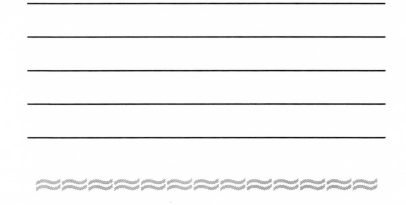

# A Near Accident

**Purpose: To recognize the influence of our beliefs**

**What's Needed?**

→ 5 uninterrupted minutes

→ A quiet place to sit

→ A pencil or pen

**Instructions:**

1. Sit quietly and breathe deeply for one minute.

2. Read the paragraph below and answer the

questions that follow by writing the first thing that comes to mind.

3. Imagine that you are driving home after a long, hot day at work. You feel relieved to exit the freeway one-half mile from your home, leaving the bottle-neck of traffic behind. You cross a major intersection, looking forward to being home and changing from business clothes into comfortable shorts and sandals, when the car coming toward you suddenly turns left in front of you. You slam on the brakes, barely avoiding a crash. Shaken, you pull over and stop your car to give yourself a moment to recover. You look in your rear-view mirror and see that the other driver has pulled over and is running toward your car. You jump out.

What do you say to the other driver? (Write the first thing that comes to your mind.)

_____

_____

_____

_____

Reread the scenario above. Imagine that the other driver runs up to you and says, "I'm so sorry. I was upset and distracted after visiting my wife. She has Alzheimer's, and I just put her in the new facility down the street."

What do you say to the other driver? (Write the first thing that comes to your mind.)

_____

_____

_____

_____

_____

Reread the scenario above. Imagine that the other driver walks up to you, and you see that the other driver is about sixteen years old, has a wireless earpiece, and is talking to someone on a cell phone.

What do you say to the other driver? (Write the first thing that comes to your mind.)

_____

_____

_____

_____

_____

**Learning Questions:**

Did you say the same thing to the other driver in the three scenarios? Why or why not?

_____

_____

_____

Did you express a pure observation (for example, "When I saw you turn left in front of me without signaling, I...") to the other driver in any of the three scenarios? If not, how did what you say differ from a pure observation?

_____

_____

_____

_____

If you expressed judgment, criticism, or blame to the other driver, restate your comment as a pure observation.

_____

_____

_____

_____

# Observing What Triggers You

**Purpose: To distinguish observation mixed with evaluation, judgment, interpretation, and blame from pure observation (free of evaluation, judgment, interpretation, and blame)**

## What's Needed?

→ 15 uninterrupted minutes

→ A pencil or pen

## Instructions:

1. Think of an interaction that left you aggravated, angry, upset, frustrated, or afraid.

What triggered you in the interaction? Specify your observation (what you saw the other do or heard the other say that pushed your buttons).

_____

_____

_____

_____

If a video tape had recorded the interaction, what pure observation would another person make about the interaction by watching the video? Be as specific and detailed as possible.

_____

_____

_____

What messages are you giving yourself (your self-talk) about the interaction?

_____

_____

_____

_____

**Learning Questions:**

Is your observation free of interpretation, judgment, evaluation, and blame?

_____

_____

How might the observation of another person watching a video of the interaction differ from yours?

_____

_____

_____

Is your self-talk about the interaction free of interpretation, judgment, evaluation, and blame?

_____

# Listening for Understanding

**Purpose: To listen for understanding**

**What's Needed?**

→ Friends, acquaintances, or coworkers to engage in conversation

**Instructions:**

1. Once each day for the next seven days, listen to another person solely to understand what's important to that person, without interrupting, interpreting,

judging, or criticizing. Cultivate openness by being curious. Silently guess the person's feelings and needs.

**Learning Questions:**

What do you observe about your way of listening in this activity compared with the way you typically listen?

_____

_____

_____

When you were listening, what were you saying to yourself (your self-talk)? For example, did you notice yourself disagreeing, criticizing, or thinking of questions to ask?

_____

What would be your reaction if you were listened to without interruption, interpretation, judgment, or criticism?

_____

_____

_____

# Feelings

*So when you are listening to somebody, completely, attentively, then you are listening not only to the words, but also to the feeling of what is being conveyed, to the whole of it, not part of it.*
—J. Krishnamurti

Let's replay my check-in at the San Francisco Airport that I described on pages 57–58, this time focusing on one part of my internal reaction that was triggered by what I saw and heard (my observations) and thought: my feelings.

When I observed approximately fifty people in front of us in line, I felt worried that we would not make our flight.

I thought we'd need a lot of luck to catch our flight, even if we were able to rush through check-in and security. This thought triggered my anxiety.

When I saw the agent waving over the agent-in-training to check us in, I felt apprehensive and doubtful about our chances of catching our flight.

When I saw the agent-in-training log on to the computer and then reach for our tickets with her hand trembling, I thought, "Just our luck to get someone who doesn't know what she's doing." With that thought, I felt aggravated.

Ten minutes later, when I thought our check-in was taking too long, I felt frustrated. After another minute passed without any apparent progress, I felt irate.

When I saw the agent-in-training continue to squint at the computer screen without moving, I felt hostile.

# What Are Feelings and Why Are They Important?

Feelings are our internal, physiological, automatic reactions to what we observe, and to what we think about our observations. Feelings are universal. We all react with feelings; they are operating in the background whether or not we are aware of them. Because every human being experiences feelings, the language of feelings helps us to connect with and relate to one another.

As shown in Figure 1 (page 5), both our observations and our thinking about what we see and hear trigger an internal, physiological reaction. The feelings we experience differ depending on whether the underlying fundamental need is met or not met by what we observe.

For example, suppose that you were born and raised in New York City, and the only time you have seen a snake was at the glass-enclosed display at the zoo. If a snake slithered across the floor of your home a few feet from you as you sit reading this book, you might feel terrified because you need physical safety. In this case, you might run from the room.

If, however, you were raised with siblings who frequently took you on walks along a river, with the goal of capturing snakes to examine under a microscope, and they taught you to appreciate the different markings on the snake's skin, how they shed, and what they eat, then you might feel curious and want to know more about the snake that is making its way across the room. You might cautiously step closer to the snake for a better look, because you need information to figure out what type of snake it is and to determine whether or not it's dangerous.

Finally, if you grew up in the foothills of Colorado, where snakes are prevalent, and your parents taught you to respect snakes because they are not aggressive and will strike only if you startle them, then you might feel sad to see a snake out of its natural environment, and need to contribute to its well-being by setting it free a safe distance from your home. You might either call the local volunteer fire department for help to safely remove it, or look in the garage for a long-handled shovel you can use to carefully lift and carry the snake outside.

In all three experiences, the observation (a snake slithering toward you from across the room) is identical. But the feelings that arise vary from terror to curiosity to sadness due to the different underlying needs (needs for physical safety, information, and protection for the well-being of the snake) that come alive in response to the observation (the snake). The specific need you experience in reaction to the snake depends on multiple factors, including your past experiences, your beliefs, your current stress level, your physical and mental health, and your thoughts about the snake.

When we are aware of the underlying need, we can then request a strategy or solution that we hope will meet our need. Imagine that the three experiences in reaction to the snake occurred in three different people, all in the same room. In response to the snake, the person needing physical safety made a request of himself to leave the room; the person needing information requested of herself to move carefully toward the snake for a closer look; the person needing protection for the well-being of the snake found the long-handled shovel and used it to carefully move the snake outside.

Others are more likely to say "yes" to our request if our Intention is to formulate a solution that will meet the others' needs as well as our own. If the three people in the room together with the snake had understood each other's needs, the person needing protection for the snake might have asked the person needing information if she would keep an eye on the snake while he escorted the person needing physical safety from the room as he headed for the garage to find the shovel.

# Feelings and Emotional Intelligence

While some of us are very much in touch with our feelings, others are detached from conscious awareness of their feelings, and experience only emotional numbness. We may disconnect from our feelings if we are criticized for being "too sensitive" or "too emotional," or if we believe that our feelings are "inappropriate," or if we psychologically shut down to protect our self from the painful aftermath of a traumatic life event.

Many years ago, I met with a therapist, a family friend whom I trusted. After listening to me complain about my life and the relationship I was in, he said to me, "You're angry." I didn't feel angry. In fact, at the time, I felt nothing at all. I replied, "No, I'm not." "Yes, you are," he continued. "You've just told me that after seeing your friends eat, within a span of ten minutes, the Greek dinner you spent three days preparing, you'll never again spend that much time cooking a meal for anyone, no matter how much you care about them. As you've been talking, I've been noticing your arms crossed in front of your chest, your left knee is crossed over your right knee, and you're swinging your left foot forward and back, forward and back. You sound and look angry to me." As I saw myself through his eyes, I became aware of the tension in my forehead, jaw, neck, shoulders, and stomach. In that moment, I realized, "Oh, so this is what anger feels like!"

We all react internally to what we observe. When we react without using emotional intelligence (EI)—without consciously identifying our feelings and then choosing our response—our feelings drive our behavior. Rather than acting with conscious choice, from the more highly evolved part of the human brain, we act out of our lower animal brain. When we react with anger, without choosing our response, we are likely to trigger either withdrawal or aggression in another.

## Reacting without consciously choosing our words sounds like this, for example:

### Father to teenage son:

*"You inconsiderate moron. How many times do I have to tell you not to eat the food I've prepared for dinner when you come home hungry from school? Are you*

*deaf? I work hard during the day, and even though I was bone-tired, I stayed up last night to fix tonight's dinner so we could eat at a decent hour. And what do you do? You come home and eat anything you want without any regard for anyone else."*

**Teenage son:**

*"I was hungry. How was I supposed to know that you didn't want me to eat what was in the fridge?"*

When we are conscious of our internal reaction and can identify our feelings, we then have the capacity of conscious choice. With practice, we can choose to use the information provided by our EI to interrupt our biologically programmed reaction. Instead of fight, flight, or freeze, we can choose how we want to respond, adversarially or non-adversarially.

When we choose to express our own emotional reaction using NAC, we first marry to our Intention to create mutual understanding, then describe what we observed, then name our feeling (either silently or out loud), name the underlying need, and choose whether to make a request now or after confirming that we were clear in our communication. When we use this non-adversarial process to communicate, we are much more likely to maintain a relationship and to get our needs met without verbal violence.

## Reacting internally and consciously choosing our words sounds like this, for example:

**Father to teenage son:**

*"I see a dirty plate and silverware in the sink, and am finding only enough food for one person left from what I prepared for tonight's dinner. I feel disappointed and frustrated because I need each of us to be considerate of everyone in this family. I worked hard during the day, and stayed up last night to fix tonight's dinner so we could eat together at a decent hour. Can we talk about how we can prevent this situation from happening again?"*

**Teenage son:**

*"I guess so."*

Feelings are pointers or cues that let us know whether our underlying needs are met or unmet. For this reason, it's helpful to expand our vocabulary of feeling words in order to use NAC. Having a vocabulary of feeling words is similar to having on hand ingredients for cooking. If you have only flour, sugar, eggs, and butter, you are limited in what you can create to meet your own or others' needs for sustenance. However, if you also have available salt, pepper, chocolate, cheese, tomatoes, and onions, you can prepare many more satisfying dishes.

The more feeling words in your vocabulary, the more you can recognize—and connect with—your own and others' internal reactions.

# What Are Words That Convey Feelings?

To express pure feelings, we use words that describe an internal reaction to what we observe without mixing in any interpretation, evaluation, blame, or other judgmental thoughts. For example, had I known NAC, instead of blaming the airline agent by saying, "You're training at our expense. We're going to miss our flight..," I would have married to my Intention and said, "When I see you staring at the computer and I know our flight is scheduled to leave in thirty minutes (observation), I feel very apprehensive about missing our flight. Can you tell me if there's a problem and whether there's anything you can do to speed up our check-in?"

The examples of feelings listed on the next page are what we may experience when our fundamental needs (such as independence, connection, celebration, meaning, integrity, and physical well-being) are met. This list is not intended to be complete.

The examples of feelings listed on the subsequent page are what we may experience when our fundamental needs (such as independence, connection, celebration, meaning, integrity, and physical well-being) are not met. The list is not intended to be complete.

# Feelings Likely When Fundamental Needs Are Being Satisfied

## Energetic
Adventurous
Alert
Alive
Aroused
Buoyant
Eager
Effervescent
Electrified
Enlivened
Enthusiastic
Excited
Exhilarated
Exuberant
Free
Impish
Intense
Invigorated
Mischievous
Playful
Refreshed
Stimulated
Thrilled
Wide-awake
Zestful

## Glad
Cheerful
Delighted
Ecstatic
Elated
Exalted
Gay
Giddy
Gleeful
Glorious
Good-humored
Grateful

Happy
Jubilant
Mirthful
Overjoyed
Pleasant
Pleased
Proud
Radiant
Rapturous
Satisfied
Thankful
Wonderful

## Hopeful
Encouraged
Expectant
Optimistic

## Intrigued
Absorbed
Amazed
Astonished
Curious
Dazzled
Engrossed
Fascinated
Inquisitive
Interested
Involved
Spellbound
Surprised

## Loving
Affectionate
Amorous
Appreciative
Compassionate
Expansive
Friendly
Helpful
Inspired
Moved
Nurtured
Pleasure
Tender
Touched
Warm

## Peaceful
Calm
Comfortable
Complacent
Composed
Confident
Content
Fulfilled
Mellow
Quiet
Relaxed
Relieved
Safe
Secure
Serene
Tranquil
Trusting

# Feelings Likely When Fundamental Needs Are Not Being Satisfied

## Confused
Ambivalent
Ashamed
Baffled
Bewildered
Dazed
Embarrassed
Hesitant
Lost
Mystified
Overwhelmed
Perplexed
Puzzled
Surprised
Torn
Troubled
Uncomfortable

## Disconnected
Alienated
Aloof
Apathetic
Bored
Detached
Distant
Distracted
Indifferent
Inert
Numb
Removed
Spiritless
Uninterested
Withdrawn

## Mad
Aggravated
Agitated
Angry
Annoyed
Bitter
Cold, Cool
Cross
Disgruntled
Disgusted

Displeased
Disquieted
Disturbed
Edgy
Enraged
Exasperated
Frustrated
Hostile
Hot
Impatient
Infuriated
Irate
Irked
Irritated
Keyed-up
Pessimistic
Resentful
Tense
Vexed

## Sad
Anguish
Brokenhearted
Despair
Desperate
Despondent
Discouraged
Disheartened
Dismayed
Distressed
Downcast
Downhearted
Gloomy
Grief
Hopeless
Hurt
Lonely
Melancholy
Mopey
Sorrowful
Sorry
Unhappy
Upset
Woeful

## Scared
Afraid
Alarmed
Anxious
Apprehensive
Breathless
Concerned
Dread
Fearful
Frightened
Helpless
Horrified
Jittery
Mistrustful
Nervous
Panicky
Petrified
Shaky
Startled
Suspicious
Tense
Terrified
Uneasy
Unnerved
Worried

## Tired
Exhausted
Fatigued
Heavy
Lethargic
Listless
Sleepy
Weary

# What Are Words That Sound Like but Are Not Feelings?

Unfortunately, it's common to use words that sound like feelings but are actually judgmental thoughts in disguise. For example, rather than expressing a pure internal, physiological reaction to what we observed (e.g., "When I hear you call me lazy, I feel hurt..."), an expression such as "I feel _____ "(fill in the blank with any of the following: betrayed, discounted, disrespected, distrusted, ignored, manipulated, misunderstood, rejected) actually describes what we think someone else is doing to us.

Although most of us think that others "make us feel" one way or another, in the NAC process, what we observe or what we think stimulates our internal feeling reactions—and the specific feeling that arises is caused by the underlying fundamental need that is either met or unmet in the situation. Others (e.g., our mother, our neighbor, our teenage son, a snake) are not the cause of our feelings. Three people in an identical situation may react very differently—one feeling scared, another feeling exhilarated, the third feeling numb—depending on their respective past experiences, beliefs, and thoughts. Although others may do or say things that stimulate a reaction in us, our met or unmet human needs are what cause us to feel one way or another in that situation.

Much of our everyday language reinforces an underlying assumption of "I'm right and you're wrong." When we believe we are describing how we feel but express our judgmental thoughts that blame others for how we feel, we distract ourselves from paying attention to our internal experience. We also are likely to elicit a defensive or an adversarial reaction, often without awareness of having triggered such a reaction.

We frequently say "I feel" and follow it with a thought. Phrases such as "I feel that..." or "I feel as if..." presuppose that we are about to reveal how we feel, but instead they end with a thought. These communications are likely to trigger a defensive reaction. Similarly, it's common to use words that sound like feelings but are actually evaluative and judgmental thoughts we make about others (e.g., "I feel you betrayed me") or about ourselves. For example, when we say "I feel _____" (fill in the blank with any of the following: ignorant, incompetent, stupid, worthless), we are expressing how we think of ourselves rather than how we feel.

If we think about ourselves in these critical terms, we are not meeting our own needs for respect, empathy, kindness, and self-acceptance. If we habitually criticize our self, we may effectively distract our self from fully experiencing our feelings, but we still are likely to feel unhappy, bitter, hopeless, withdrawn, numb, or weary—feelings that come up when our fundamental human needs are not met.

# Key Learning Points

→ Feelings are our internal, physiological, automatic reactions to what we see or hear, and to our thoughts about what we see or hear.

Feelings are present even when we are not consciously aware of them.

→ Because every human being experiences feelings, the language of feelings helps us to relate to and connect with one another.

→ When we react without using our emotional intelligence (EI)—without consciously iden- tifying our feelings and then choosing our response—our feelings drive our behavior. When we are able to identify our feelings, we have the capacity of conscious choice. With conscious choice, we can interrupt our automatic reaction of fight, flight, or freeze, marry to our Intention, and then choose how we want to respond, before we say or do anything we might regret.

→ Feelings are pointers or cues that let us know whether our underlying needs are met or unmet. The more feeling words in our vo- cabulary, the easier it is to identify our own and others' internal reactions.

→ It's common to use words that sound like feelings but are actually judgmental thoughts in disguise.

The following activities are designed to create awareness of feelings in yourself and others.

# Learning Activities to Deepen Emotional Intelligence for Feelings

## Identifying Your Feelings

**Purpose: To experience our internal, physiological reactions (our feelings)**

**What's Needed?**

→ 5 uninterrupted minutes

→ A quiet place to sit

→ Paper

→ A pencil or pen

→ A timer

→ Optional: the feelings lists (pages 91–92)

**Instructions:**

1. Set the timer for three minutes.

2. Sit quietly and breathe deeply for one minute. Your eyes may be open or closed as you prefer. Continue to breathe deeply as you turn your attention inward.

3. Focus your attention on your feelings.

4. Check in with yourself at least six times over the next two minutes, and each time write down what you are feeling. Use the feelings lists if necessary.

5. Stop when the timer goes off.

Feelings I experience over a two-minute time period:

_____

_____

_____

**Learning Questions:**

Read what you wrote down as your internal experience.

What, if anything, that you wrote down surprises you?

_____

_____

_____

Did your feelings change over the two minutes? If yes, what do you think led your feelings to change? (Hint: Did you shift your thoughts or your attention?)

_____

_____

_____

Are all the feelings you identified included on one of the two lists of pure feelings? Circle one: YES / NO

If you circled NO, list the words you wrote down that are not on the feelings lists:

_____

_____

_____

_____

_____

Now let's examine whether those words express a pure internal experience (feeling) or a critical thought.

If you say to another person, "My reaction to what you said (or did) is that I feel _____" (insert one word that you wrote down that is not on the feelings lists), is the other person likely to respond with irritation or with caring?

_____

Repeat this activity using each word that you wrote down that is not on the feelings lists.

In your heart-of-hearts, do you think it's the other person's fault if you react as described by the particular word that's not on the feelings lists? For example, if you say, "I feel invalidated," do you tend to blame the other person for doing something that "makes" you feel that way?

_____

**Learning Points:**

Feelings usually change every few seconds or minutes in response to where we focus our attention.

Feelings are present and are influencing how we express ourselves even when we are not consciously aware of them.

If we say "I feel" followed by a word that is not a pure feeling, and the other person reacts with irritation or defensiveness—and if we believe that the other person is to blame for our emotional response—then we probably used a word that sounds like a feeling but is a judgment in disguise.

# Recognizing Another's Feelings

**Purpose: To recognize another's internal, physiological reactions (feelings)**

## What's Needed?

→ 10 uninterrupted minutes

→ A movie on DVD or video

→ A timer

## Instructions:

1. As you watch a movie, observe an actor in a scene and guess what the actor is feeling.

2. Stop the movie and ask yourself: "What do I hear that actor say and see that actor do that leads me to conclude that the actor is experiencing that feeling?" Write down your pure observations of what you hear and see that conveys the feeling to you.

_____

_____

_____

_____

_____

_____

_____

**Suggestions:**

Repeat this activity, observing another actor in the same movie or in a different movie.

_____

_____

_____

_____

Repeat this activity, observing a real person in the moment.

_____

_____

_____

_____

≈≈≈≈≈≈≈≈≈≈≈≈≈≈≈≈≈≈≈≈≈

# Needs

*Acceptance of our own self is the first step to connecting with another.*

*—Leigh Fountain*

L et's once again revisit my check-in at the San Francisco Airport that I described on pages 57–58, this time focusing on the second part of my internal reaction: my needs. As illustrated in Figure 1 (page 5), my observations and my thoughts stimulated my internal reactions—my feelings and my needs—as described below.

When I observed approximately fifty people in front of us in line, I felt worried that we wouldn't make our flight, because I needed the comfort of being home.

I thought we'd need a lot of luck to catch our flight, even if we were able to rush through check-in and security. This thought triggered my anxiety because I needed a restful pace.

When I saw the agent wave over the agent-in-training to check us in, I felt apprehensive and pessimistic about our chances of catching our flight, because I needed efficiency.

When I saw the agent-in-training log on to the computer and then reach with a trembling hand for our tickets, I thought, "Just our luck to get someone who doesn't know what she's doing." With that thought, I felt aggravated because I needed efficiency and accuracy.

Ten minutes later, when I thought our check-in was taking too long, I felt frustrated. After another minute passed without any apparent progress, I felt irate because I needed information.

When I saw the agent-in-training continue to squint at the computer screen without moving, I felt hostile because I needed understanding and reassurance.

# What Are Needs and Why Are They Important?

Unfortunately, many people mistakenly believe that to have needs means to be "needy," deficient, or lacking in some quality. In NAC, needs mean something quite different.

Needs are our deepest, most fundamental human yearnings for qualities that would enrich our life and enable us to thrive. When our needs—such as those for physical well-being (e.g., food, water), autonomy (independence), interdependence (social relationships and connection), integrity, and meaning—are met, our life energy lifts up, strengthens, and radiates. When our needs are unmet, our life energy diminishes. At the airport, the needs that came alive in me were unmet, and my unmet needs gave rise to cheerless energy, producing worry, anxiety, apprehension, aggravation, and hostility.

Because needs are inborn and universal, all human beings have them, including every need listed on page 110—and those needs are also individual, depending on the circumstances.

The needs that come alive for me in a given situation may

not be the needs that come alive for you in the same situation, as illustrated by the snake scenario on pages 84–86. As another example, suppose we work for the same person, and during our regular staff meeting, we hear our boss take credit for work that we've each done. Upon hearing our boss's words, I may feel angry or disgusted because my needs for integrity, appreciation, respect, and honesty in my work environment are not being met. In order to meet my needs, I might look for another job. You, on the other hand, may feel pleased, perhaps because you interpret our boss's actions to mean that your work is of the highest quality, so you feel content to remain in your job, because you need job security.

Although every human being has fundamental needs, many of us lack awareness of our needs and the vocabulary to express them, because we are socialized to ignore our needs. Males, for example, are traditionally raised to believe that to show emotion and to have needs is to be weak. Females, on the other hand, are traditionally socialized to put everyone else's needs before their own. When we lack awareness of our own needs, we are disconnected from knowing our full identity as a human being.

When we have not developed our emotional intelligence, we react and may make decisions without conscious awareness of how our emotions are driving those decisions. Decisions made without conscious emotional and intellectual alignment may not be in our own best interest.

For example, we mediated a divorce between spouses who were locked in a bitter conflict over parenting time and decision-making authority for their children, and over dividing up assets and debts. After several contentious meetings, and with the mediator's assistance to get back on track after numerous flare-ups, they were able to come to several agreements. After a two-week break, they returned for another meeting. Much to our surprise, the wife began backing away from the financial agreements they had struggled to reach.

As a side comment, the wife mentioned that she had been in a traffic accident between the last meeting and the current session. We asked her to describe what had happened.

**Wife:**

*"I was stopped at a traffic light and suddenly saw a car coming from behind without slowing down. I don't know what the driver was doing but he rear-ended me. I don't think he ever applied his brakes. Thank goodness our children weren't with me."*

**Mediator:**

*"When you think about being in that accident, I'm guessing that you feel scared and vulnerable, and that you need safety and security. Is that true?"*

**Wife (after a brief pause):**

*"Yes. I was shaking badly when the police arrived, but fortunately I was able to walk away without any serious injuries. My car is totaled though. So now I'm left dealing with the insurance company, and I have to figure out what to do for a car."*

**Mediator:**

*"It sounds like you are feeling alone, without a back-up, and you need security and support right now. Is my understanding accurate?"*

**Wife: (with tears in her eyes, silently nods "yes.")**

Once she connected to her feelings and needs, the wife calmly reviewed the financial agreements they had made in previous meetings, and realized she felt comfortable with the decisions they had made. She then was willing to move on to discussing the remaining issues.

When we have not developed our emotional intelligence, we are more likely to either resist, rebel, or live to please others. When we live in reaction to the needs of others, we allow others to define how we live our lives, rather than live in integrity with ourselves.

# What Are Words That Identify Needs?

The list of needs on the next page is based on multiple sources, including the book *Nonviolent Communication* by Marshall Rosenberg. The list presents the fundamental human needs of autonomy, connection/interdependence, celebration, integrity, meaning, peace, and physical well-being, together with many terms we commonly use to express these needs. This list is intended to be illustrative rather than definitive.

# Needs

## Autonomy
Choice
Freedom
Independence
Space
Spontaneity

## Connection/ Interdependence
Acceptance/Self-acceptance
Acknowledgment
Affection
Appreciation
Belonging
Closeness
Commitment
Community
Companionship
Compassion
Connection
Consideration
Consistency
Contribution to the enrichment of life
Cooperation
Emotional Safety
Empathy
Fairness
Feedback that empowers and enables
  us to learn from our limitations
Help
Inclusion
Intimacy
Kindness
Love
Nurturing
Reassurance
Recognition
Respect/Self-respect
Safety/Security
Self-expression
Self-worth
Support
To know and be known
Trust
Understanding
Warmth

## Celebration
Joy
Humor
Play
To celebrate losses and gains

## Integrity
Alignment
Authenticity
Creativity
Honesty
Presence

## Meaning
Awareness
Clarity
Competence
Consciousness
Effectiveness
Growth
Mourning
Purpose
Wisdom

## Peace
Beauty
Communion
Ease
Equality
Harmony
Inspiration
Order
Spirituality
Stability

## Physical Well-Being
Air
Exercise/movement
Food
Physical safety
Protection from life-threatening forms
  of life: viruses, bacteria, insects,
    predatory animals and human beings
Rest
Sexual expression
Shelter
Touch
Water

A need identifies an internal hunger or yearning for a quality of life, without specifying how, by whom, by when, or where we would like the need to be met. These yearnings—for meaning or purpose, for relationship, for the freedom to make our own choices, etc.—are separate from the requests we make (strategies we propose) to meet our needs. When we mix up our needs with the requests that we think will meet our needs, we are expressing our attachment to a specific option for meeting our need.

## For example:

### Mixing need with request:
*"It snowed over twenty inches last night, and I need you to shovel the driveway."*

### Separating need from request:
*"It snowed over twenty inches last night, and I'm feeling overwhelmed and need help. Would you be willing to shovel the driveway?"*

### Mixing need with request:
*"I have two weeks of vacation coming up next month. I need us to go to Hawaii for some R and R."*

### Separating need from request:
*"I have two weeks of vacation coming up next month, and I need play and relaxation. Would you enjoy spending two weeks on a beach with me?"*

**Mixing need with request:**

*"I need to be paid for the concert tickets before the bank closes at 3:00 this afternoon."*

**Separating need from request:**

*"I paid for the concert tickets and feel worried because I overdrew my account and need financial security. Can you pay me back before 3:00 this afternoon so that I can deposit the money today?"*

Not only does mixing needs with our requests for meeting our needs limit the possible ways to get our needs met, when we mix the two, the other person is much more likely to resist or react defensively. In other words, we are likely to trigger a conflict.

# Emotional Intelligence and Fundamental Needs

Having emotional intelligence (EI) means that we are able to identify and experience our fundamental needs. EI provides us with the information that enables us to consciously take responsibility for meeting our needs and for the quality of our relationships with others. Even when we are unaware of our needs, they influence how we feel and how we react.

When we are disconnected from and do not take responsibility for knowing our needs, we often communicate them indirectly by expressing our judgmental thoughts through criticism, judgment, and blame of others. In human interactions, if we focus on solutions without identifying our unmet needs, we inadvertently create disconnection and increase the likelihood of mistakes and conflicts.

For example, when we are disconnected from our own needs, we react from the feelings that come up when our needs are not met, as I had done at the airport. We blame others for our inner state, criticizing and blaming when things don't go as we'd like. We say, for example: "It's your fault that I'm so unhappy." "You do that just to make me angry." "You must think I'm stupid." "If you loved me, you would..." "You're training at our expense. We're going to miss our flight."

When we are out of touch with our needs, and the needs of others, we tend to come up with solutions to problems without fully understanding and addressing what's truly important to those involved. For example, I directed the agent-in-training to "Get some help now!" without knowing whether she needed help or simply needed time for a slow computer to process our reservation. A solution must meet at least some of the needs of all concerned in order to have the highest probability of success.

When we are disconnected from our needs, we are disconnected from an inner voice that guides us by speaking through the inner experience of our feelings. Our needs express themselves through our feelings—for example, joy or comfort when our needs are met, and sadness, fear, or anger when our needs are unmet (see feelings lists on pages 91–92).

I've learned, for example, that whenever I feel tension in my upper chest, just above my heart, and "butterflies" in the area of my heart, I'm feeling anxious and it's time for me to stop and ask myself what I'm observing and needing. Anxiety is my cue that a need is trying to get my attention. Identifying what I'm observing and needing allows me to reconnect to myself.

# Language and Phrasing

Because the feelings we experience are caused by our own underlying needs rather than by another person, when we hold the Intention to nurture a relationship, one way to begin the communication process is to use the phrase "When I see you do _____ (or hear you say _____), I feel _____ because I need _____."

Although this simple phrasing may sound awkward at first, it directs our attention inward toward our own feelings and needs, and interrupts our tendency toward judgmental thinking expressed as outward criticism and blame.

When we choose to listen for understanding, it is essential to remember that the speaker is the expert on her own internal experience, but she probably doesn't know what she needs. For this reason, as explained more fully on page 27, we offer a guess as a reference point for the speaker to shift her attention inward, and we invite correction if our understanding does not match her experience, as shown below.

After listening to the speaker, we pause for as long as necessary to marry to Intention. Then we confirm our understanding of what we heard by using phrases such as "When you see or hear or remember \_\_\_\_\_, do you feel \_\_\_\_\_ because you need \_\_\_\_\_?" or "When you see or hear or remember \_\_\_\_\_, I'm guessing that you might feel \_\_\_\_\_ because you need \_\_\_\_\_. Is that accurate?"

Once the other person feels heard, we either choose to express our self or to ask if the other has a request for how to meet the identified need.

## Key Learning Points

→ Needs are our deepest, most fundamental human yearnings for qualities that would enrich our life and enable us to thrive.

→ A need does not specify how, by whom, by when, or where we would like the need to be met.

→ Because needs are inborn and universal, every human being has them. The needs that come alive for one person in a given situation may not be the needs that come alive for others in the same situation. In that sense, needs are individual as well as universal.

→ In NAC, to have needs does not mean to be "needy," deficient, or lacking.

→ When our needs are met, our life energy is enhanced. When our needs are unmet, our life energy is diminished.

→ When we are disconnected from our needs, we often communicate our needs indirectly through our judgmental thoughts expressed as criticism, judgment, and blame.

→ When we hold the Intention to nurture a relationship, one way to begin is to communicate by using the phrase "When I see you do _____ (or hear you say _____), I feel _____ because I need _____."

→ When we choose to listen for understanding, it is important to guess the speaker's feelings and needs because it gives her a reference point, and because the speaker is the expert on her own internal experience.

# Learning Activities to Deepen Emotional Intelligence for Needs

## Becoming Acquainted with Your Needs

**Purpose: To experience your needs**

### What's Needed?

→ 15 uninterrupted minutes

→ The needs list (page 110)

→ A pencil or pen

### Instructions:

1. Read the needs list slowly, either out loud or silently, noting any internal sensation of resonating, even longing, for one or more of the needs to be met. Do not rush through this exercise. Stay with any sense of resonating to allow yourself to experience the need(s) for which you feel some energy. Simply breathe deeply for a few seconds, and stay with the energy for at least thirty seconds before continuing.

**Learning Questions:**

Are there one or more needs that frequently come alive for you? If yes, which ones?

_____

_____

Specifically, what do you see someone doing or hear someone saying, or what are you telling yourself, that brought that need alive for you?

_____

_____

_____

_____

When you recall these situations, how do you feel?

_____

_____

When your need is not met in these situations, what do you tell yourself?

_____

_____

_____

What strategy do you use to try to meet this need?

_____

_____

How well is this strategy working for you?

_____

What alternative strategies can you think of?

_____

_____

_____

_____

**Suggestion:**

Repeat this exercise, focusing on what needs are met and unmet for you in one specific context: at work, at home, or in a relationship.

# Owning Your Needs

**Purpose: To identify your motivation behind your actions**

### What's Needed?

→ 15 uninterrupted minutes

→ The needs list (page 110)

→ A pencil or pen

### Instructions:

1. On the chart on the next page, list up to ten things you say you do because you "have to" (for example, pay taxes, clean the bathroom).

### Things I say I do because I "have to."

1.

2.

3.

4.

5.

6.

7.

8.

9.

10.

2. For each thing you listed as doing because you "have to," use the needs list (page 110) to identify all the possible needs you meet when you engage in these activities.

**For example:**

I do _____ (pay taxes) because that meets my needs for _____(freedom, contribution to community, and honesty).

**Hint:** For ease, you may wish to copy your list of things you say you do because you "have to" into the left column in the chart on the next page.

| Things I say I do because I "have to." | I do _____ because that meets my needs for _____. |
|---|---|
| 1. | 1. |
| 2. | 2. |
| 3. | 3. |
| 4. | 4. |
| 5. | 5. |
| 6. | 6. |
| 7. | 7. |
| 8. | 8. |
| 9. | 9. |
| 10. | 10. |

**Learning Questions:**

How do you feel when you say "I have to" compared with when you express the needs you are meeting by doing those activities?

_____

_____

_____

Does the shift in your language shift your attitude or motivation? If so, how?

_____

_____

_____

_____

**Suggestion:**

Ask a friend to tell you up to ten things he does because he "has to." Then guess the needs he might be meeting by engaging in those activities.

# Expressing Gratitude

**Purpose: To fully express your feeling of gratitude to another**

## What's Needed?

→ 20 uninterrupted minutes

→ The needs list (page 110)

→ A pencil or pen

## Instructions:

1. Using the formal structure of observation, feeling, need, and request (if one), express in writing three gratitudes you feel toward others.

   **For example:** "When I see you throw your clothes in the hamper, I feel grateful because I'm working long hours and your picking up your clothes meets my need for support right now." Or: "I appreciate when you throw your clothes in the hamper because that meets my need for support while I'm working long hours."

   _____

   _____

   _____

   _____

_____

_____

_____

_____

2. Express at least one feeling of gratitude that you feel for yourself.

_____

_____

_____

3. Think of someone who does things that upset you. What appreciation can you express for that person? Be sure to include the need that was met for you as part of your expression of appreciation.

**For example:**

_"When my friend is thirty minutes later than he said he would be, I feel upset because I need commitments to be honored. However, I appreciate that when he is late, he's helping me to learn to be flexible."_

_____

_____

_____

_____

_____

_____

_____

4. Express appreciation using NAC to one of the people you identified in Step 1. Remember to include the need that was met for you by the other's actions.

**Learning Questions:**

What's one appreciation that you long to hear?

_____

_____

_____

_____

What need lives beneath that longing?

_____

What do you observe about your reaction to this activity?

_____

_____

_____

How challenging or easy is it for you to feel gratitude for yourself compared with feeling it for someone or something else?

_____

_____

_____

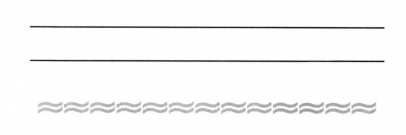

## Giving Feedback

**Purpose: To give feedback in a way likely to be understood**

**What's Needed?**

→ 15 uninterrupted minutes

→ The feelings lists (pages 91–92)

→ The needs list (see page 110)

→ A pencil or pen

**Instructions:**

1. Think of two situations where someone did or said something you did not enjoy.

2. In the two columns on the next page, one for each situation, write down your pure observations.

**#1 Pure Observations**

_____

_____

_____

_____

_____

_____

**#2 Pure Observations**

_____

_____

_____

_____

_____

_____

3. Answer the following questions for the situation in the left column.

What is your Intention for this relationship? What kind of relationship do you want to create?

_____

_____

_____

When you think of what the person said or did, how do you feel?

_____

_____

What need in you was unmet?

_____

_____

What do you wish the person had done differently that might have met your need?

_____

_____

_____

What is your request of yourself? Do you wish to give feedback in this situation? If not, how can you meet your need without involving the other?

_____

_____

_____

_____

If you wish to involve the other person, what might he need?

_____

_____

4. Repeat Steps 1–4 for the situation in the right column.

What is your Intention for this relationship? What kind of relationship do you want to create?

_____

_____

_____

When you think of what the person said or did, how do you feel?

_____

_____

_____

What need in you was unmet?

_____

_____

What do you wish the person had done differently that might have met your need?

_____

_____

What is your request of yourself? Do you wish to give feedback in this situation? If not, how can you meet your need without involving the other?

_____

_____

_____

If you wish to involve the other person, what might he need?

_____

_____

**Learning Questions:**

How challenging or easy is it for you to give someone feedback when that person says or does something that you do not enjoy?

_____

What is your belief about giving feedback? Do you believe that feedback can be given honestly and kindly?

_____

_____

_____

How did you feel about this activity?

_____

_____

_____

What did you learn from this activity?

_____

_____

_____

_____

_____

≈≈≈≈≈≈≈≈≈≈≈≈≈≈≈≈≈≈≈≈

# Requests

*One effective way to ask is to be prepared to hear either a "yes" or a "no." . . . People like the freedom and power of being able to truly choose. Ask this way and you are more likely to hear a "yes."*

—Rinatta Paries

When my husband and I were checking in for our flight at the San Francisco Airport, I had many unmet needs, as described on pages 105–106, including comfort, a restful pace, efficiency, accuracy, information, understanding, and reassurance. What requests might I have made to meet those needs had I known NAC at that time?

To meet my needs for the comfort of being at home and a restful pace, I might have said to the original airline agent on duty when we arrived at the counter, "We've been in line for over forty-five minutes, and I'm worried that we'll have to rush to catch our flight. I'm guessing that you need a break, but would you be willing to stay here long enough to be sure that the agent-in-training is able to quickly check us in?"

To meet my needs for efficiency and accuracy, I could have asked the agent-in-training, "Our check-in is taking much longer than I had thought it would, since we have electronic tickets, and I notice that you're staring at the computer screen. I'm guessing that you might need some assistance. Can you tell me whether you're finding our reservation in the system?"

When I needed information, I might have made the

following request: "It's been over ten minutes since we started checking in. I'm guessing that you need to be very accurate, and I need to know whether there's a problem that might keep us from catching our flight. Can you give me any information to help me understand what's taking so long?"

Because I needed understanding and reassurance, I might have said, "It's been one hour since we got in line to check in, and I'm upset that we might miss our flight. I'm guessing that you need to work at a pace that keeps you from making mistakes. Could you verify how much time is left before the flight is scheduled to take off, and tell me whether you think we'll be able to get to the gate on time?"

# What Are Requests and Why Are They Important?

In the last chapter, we distinguished that a need is separate from how, by whom, by when, or where we would like that need to be met. Requests are expressed as invitations to engage in strategies—the specifics of how, by whom, by when, or where—that we predict will meet our needs.

We don't know whether or not the request we make will actually meet our need until we implement the strategy. In other words, requests are strategies that we hypothesize will leave us feeling satisfied when implemented. Sometimes we make one request, try the strategy, and then, if it doesn't meet our need, make another request, in order to bring about the resolution we seek.

Requests having the highest probability of success are those that consider and attempt to meet the needs of all involved. Depending on the situation, such as at the airport, sometimes the best we can do is to invite solutions that meet some of everyone's needs.

When we hold an Intention to understand and respect everyone's needs, then we remain open to a variety of possible solutions until there is consensus among the people involved that a workable strategy has been found. When we connect with each other through a mutual understanding of our needs, then potential solutions are limited only by our imagination and creativity. In other words, there are many possible strategies to meet a need.

If I need love and connection, for example, I may believe that any of the following strategies would meet my needs: call someone I care about once a day, get a puppy, join a singles group, volunteer at a senior center, get a massage, ask someone out to dinner, take up ballroom dancing, seek companionship through an Internet dating service, register for an adult education class, participate in an Internet chat room, join a ski or hiking club, become involved in a community garden, or start a book club. A request is an invitation to engage in one or several strategies in order to alleviate the pain of an unmet need.

## What Gets in the Way?

Many things either hold us back from making requests, or make it unlikely that our requests will be granted, including our fears, lack of clarity, and our habits of adversarial communication, as described below.

**Fear of Vulnerability:** It takes courage to request the strategy we think will meet our need. It's not unusual to feel vulnerable when we reveal our needs to others.

**Lack of Clarity:** A request is likely to be met with resistance when we rush to resolve a problem before gaining clear understanding of the underlying need. Often we're not accustomed to asking for what we want. We may feel uncertain because we don't know if what we request will actually meet our need. Further, many of us don't know what we want to request, because we may be clear about what we don't want but unclear about what we think will meet our need. Even when someone would enjoy helping us to meet our need, if he is unable to discern a clear request on our part, he may not know what to do. The more clear we are about what need we are trying to meet, and what we want to request to meet that need, the more likely our request will be met.

**Fear of Rejection:** In addition to feeling vulnerable and uncertain, we may feel hesitant if we made a request in the past that elicited a response that left our need unmet. The language of invitation, such as NAC, is foreign to us. Using Non-Adversarial Communication does not guarantee that our request will be granted, even when we phrase our feelings, needs, and requests correctly. NAC does give us the skills to understand what need the other person is trying to meet by saying "no" to our request, and to decide whether there is a request that will meet the needs of both.

When we first attempt to make requests in language that invites a positive response, it sometimes feels safer, especially if we are afraid of rejection, to make a request that we think the other person is likely to grant, rather than a request that actually addresses our unmet need. For example, if I need appreciation and request that you set the table, the request does not match my need for appreciation. But if I say, "I know you're hungry, but I'm wondering if you would be willing to take a moment before eating to say 'thank you' for the time I spent planning the meal, shopping for the food, and preparing the meal," then my need for appreciation is likely to be met. It is important to make a request that aligns with the need you are trying to meet.

**Making Win-Lose Requests:** When requests are stated with only one person's needs in mind, they are likely to be met with defensiveness. A win-lose solution that meets our own need while ignoring or doing harm to another is likely to provoke an adversarial reaction from the person whose need was not addressed. When requests are shaped to take into account everyone's needs, people are more likely to make agreements and to fulfill their commitments, because the proposed solution is also in their best interest.

**Making Demands:** If we are invested in a specific strategy or solution, then we are divorced from Intention. We are taking a stance that we know the best course of action, and forgetting that our request is simply a guess or prediction of what will meet our needs. When we are invested in a specific strategy, we are less likely to be taking into consideration the needs of others in addition to our own.

Further, when we are attached to a single solution, our "request" is likely to be a demand or be heard as a demand, rather than a request to consider a possibility. Because there are unlimited options for meeting needs, not being attached to any single solution means that one may refuse a request without fear of punishment. A request is an invitation, similar to an invitation to dinner.

If we invite someone to our home for dinner, we typically feel sad, disappointed, or frustrated if she declines our invitation. If we react with anger and want to teach her a lesson so she regrets saying "no," then we made a demand rather than an invitation. When we make a request in NAC and the other person says "no," if, instead of reacting with anger, we listen to understand what's important to the other person and guess at what need she is trying to meet, then we have an opportunity to reshape our request to take into account her need as well as our own.

**Mixing Need with Strategy:** We are likely to mistakenly combine a need with a strategy to meet that need, especially when we lack a vocabulary to express our needs. For example, if I say, "I need you to love me," I am mixing up my need for love with a strategy of identifying a specific person to meet my need. If that person isn't willing or able to love me, then I've left myself no other options for my need to be met. In another example, "I need you to get rid of your dog so I can sleep in peace and quiet without being awakened by barking" combines my need for peace, quiet, and uninterrupted sleep with the strategy of getting rid of your dog. When we combine a need with a strategy, our request is likely to elicit a defensive reaction from the other person, leaving us with the turmoil of conflict as well as the pain of our unmet need.

We need to practice making requests so that we can overcome holding back because we feel vulnerable, don't know what will actually meet our needs, or fear rejection. We also need to practice making requests in order to avoid reverting to habits of adversarial communication (making win-lose requests, making demands, mixing need with strategy).

# What Are the Types of Requests?

There are two types of requests: requests to invite connection and requests to invite action.

**Connection requests:** Connection requests ask for feedback to confirm whether we have expressed our observations, feelings, and needs in the easy-to-hear way we intended. They can also be requests that ask for the other person to express his reaction to what we've said. A request for reaction is an invitation to engage in conversation with us.

When we express ourselves, although we may think we've

been clear, the message we intended to send is frequently not the message that the other person has received. It is our responsibility to verify that the message has been received as we had hoped, especially when we see that our communication has elicited a reaction that we did not expect. Before we continue, we want to know that we are understood in the way we intended.

For example, "I'm not sure I'm being clear so I would like some feedback. Would you be willing to tell me your understanding of what I've said?" The other person may say something similar to what we believe we said, or may surprise us by saying something very different from what we expected. If she responds by genuinely trying to tell us what she heard, regardless of how accurate or inaccurate it may seem to us, then she is responding to our request. The appropriate response back to her, therefore, is "Thank you." When her response does not align with what we had intended to communicate, continue with "I apparently was not as clear as I had hoped. Would you be willing to allow me to take another minute to try to say it again?"

Sometimes, after we have spoken and the other person begins his response, we realize that he may not have understood what we said. When this happens, we are likely to find it difficult to listen to him, because we do not feel confident that we were understood. In this case, it's important to use NAC to express our own need to be heard in a way that also meets the other's needs. For example, "I want to understand what you're saying, but I can't really take it in because I don't feel heard and I don't know if I've expressed myself clearly. Would you please let me know what you heard me say before we continue?

People who have not learned NAC rarely make clear requests, so when we are the listener, we will probably have to prompt them for their request. For example, we might ask, "Do you have a request?" or "Is there something you would like from me?" or "Do you have any ideas for what you might want that would meet your needs?"

The second connection request invites the other person to let us know her reaction to what we expressed. Such a request might be "Would you be willing to tell me your reaction to what I've just said?" When she tells us her reaction, she is engaging with us in the dance of communication. We remain in the NAC process by listening, and by guessing her feelings and needs to confirm that we understood her reaction. In order to continue the conversation, we might say, "Would you be willing to hear my reaction to what you just said?"

**Action requests:** Action requests ask for an action to be taken that meets the needs of all involved. For example, if my car is in the shop for repairs and I'm aggravated because the friend giving me a ride to work is fifteen minutes late, then I might request of myself that I look into the bus schedule and other alternatives (e.g., getting a rental car), because I need to keep my commitment to be at work by 8:00 a.m. Or I might say to my friend, "I'm very appreciative that you are willing to pick me up, because I need help right now. I'm anxious because I made a commitment to be at work by 8:00 a.m. I would love to ride with you if you are able to pick me up by 7:30 a.m. However, if that's a problem for you, I understand and I'm willing to catch the bus so that I can be at work by 8:00."

# Characteristics of Requests

There are four characteristics of requests that reduce the chance of misunderstanding:

**Positive phrasing:** Many people tend to say what they don't want (e.g., "I don't want to be late.") rather than what they do want ("I want to be at work by 8:00 a.m."). One important characteristic of a request is that it express what we do want to happen. Often people would like to do what we ask but feel confused because they don't know what we are asking. For example, "Please don't call before 8:00 p.m. because I'll be eating dinner" does not clarify how late I can call without disturbing you.

**Specific:** It is important to phrase a request so that it is concrete. When we make our request as specific as possible, there is less likely to be misunderstanding due to ambiguity. For example, rather than "Be responsible," a specific request might be "Please be home by midnight, and either park in the garage or lock the car if you park on the street."

**Do-able:** For needs to be met, our requests must be humanly possible to carry out. For example, "I know you get off work downtown at 5:00 p.m., but are you willing to pick up our daughter at her school thirty miles away by 5:15 p.m. so that we don't have to pay extra for child care?" is unlikely to be a do-able request. Rather than shape a request that makes it impossible for needs to be met, refocus on the needs to be sure that all needs have been identified. In this example, racing across town to travel thirty miles in fifteen minutes is unlikely to meet the driver's need for safety. A request that might meet the needs for safety and financial security might be to ask another child's parent if she could pick up your daughter along with her child.

**Time-bound:** Shaping a request to have clear timing and deadlines helps people understand what they need to do in order to fulfill the request. For example, rather than "Let's meet on Thursday," a time-bound request is "Can we meet for one hour beginning at 3:00 p.m. on Thursday, December 5th, at my office."

In addition to the above ways to frame a request in order to avoid misunderstanding, it is helpful to shape our request so that it meets the most pressing need we can identify, rather than make several requests to meet several unmet needs. People tend to feel overwhelmed and resistant if we make too many requests at one time. We can often identify one or two needs that seem more alive than the others, by slowing down and allowing time to experience each need in turn. Briefly focusing on each need usually reveals that one or two resonate more strongly than the others.

When we are able to prioritize among several unmet needs,

making a request that will meet the need that is more important or pressing than the others often satisfies the others as well, at least for a while.

## Determining Whom the Request Is For

After we clarify for our self what we observed, how we feel, and what we need, and, if another is involved, confirmed our understanding of the other's reaction (feelings and needs), then we have an opportunity to choose: Do we make a request of the other person, or is there a request that we wish to make of our self in order to resolve the situation, or is it a combination of the two?

For example, if I resent my coworkers because work is handed off to me with only a few hours before the deadline for delivery to a client, I might choose to say to them, "On our last three projects, I received work from you at 4:45 that was due the next day. I worked late each time in order to meet the deadlines and our commitments, although I felt stressed and exhausted. I both want to be a supportive team member and do my best work. I would like to meet with you to talk about how we can meet our deadlines without my receiving work at the last minute, forcing me to work all night in order to get the work delivered on time to our client. Can we meet as a team to talk about this tomorrow for an hour at 1:00?"

Or I might choose to make a request of myself and not involve my coworkers. For example, instead of talking with my coworkers, I might ask myself if there is a way for me to reduce stress and do my work with integrity and competence so that it contributes to the team's success. I might request of myself to try the following strategies: I will check with team members a few days prior to the deadline to confirm the timing of the handoff of work to me. If possible, I will begin part of the work rather than wait for all of it to be passed on to me. In addition, if warranted, I will come to work later on the day I expect to work late in order to meet the deadline, so that I won't exhaust myself if I work through the night.

# Key Learning Points

→ Requests are invitations to engage in strategies that we believe will meet our needs. We won't know if the request actually meets our need until the strategy is implemented.

→ Requests that consider and attempt to meet the needs of everyone involved have the highest probability of success.

→ We hold back from making requests because we feel vulnerable, don't know what will actually meet our needs, or fear rejection. We need to practice making requests so we can overcome holding back, and so we can avoid reverting to habits of adversarial communication (making win-lose requests, making demands, mixing need with strategy).

→ There are two types of requests: requests

to invite connection and requests to invite action.

→ Requests for connection help ensure that we have been understood in the way we intended, and invite a reaction to what we have expressed. When the other person reveals his reaction, he is engaging with us in the dance of communication.

→ Requests for action ask for an action to be taken that meets the needs of all involved.

→ The clearer we are about what we need and what we would like to request to meet that need, the less likely the chance for misunderstanding. For this reason, it is important that requests are phrased in positive language expressing what we do want, and are specific, do-able, and time-bound.

→ When we experience several unmet needs, it is most beneficial to shape a request to meet the most pressing need.

→ It is important to determine whether to make a request of someone else, of our self, or of both.

# Learning Activities to Deepen Skills for Making Requests

## Making Requests of Others
**Purpose: To make requests rather than demands**

### What's Needed?

→ 10 uninterrupted minutes

→ A quiet place to sit

→ A pencil or pen

### Instructions:

1. Think of a situation in which you either want to or did make a request of another person. Briefly state:

Your Observation:

_____

_____

_____

Your Feeling(s):

_____

_____

Your Need(s):

_____

The Other Person's Need(s):

_____

Your Request:

_____

_____

_____

**Learning Questions:**

What type of request (connection or action) did you make?

_____

If you made a request for connection, was it a request for understanding, a request for reaction, or both?

_____

_____

_____

If you made a request for action, was your request:

→ Positive?

→ Specific?

→ Do-able?

→ Time-bound?

How does your request take into consideration the other person's need(s)?

_____

_____

_____

≈≈≈≈≈≈≈≈≈≈≈≈≈≈≈≈≈≈≈≈≈

# Making Requests of Yourself

**Purpose: To make requests rather than demands**

**What's Needed?**

→ 10 uninterrupted minutes

→ A quiet place to sit

→ A pencil or pen

**Instructions:**

1. Think of a situation in which you either want to or did make a request of yourself. Briefly state:

Your Observation:

_____

_____

_____

Your Feeling(s):

_____

_____

Your Need(s):

_____

The Other Person's Need(s):

_____

Your Request:

_____

_____

_____

**Learning Questions:**

What type of request did you make?

_____

If you made a request for action, was your request:

→ Positive?

→ Specific?

→ Do-able?

→ Time-bound?

How does your request take into consideration the other person's need(s)?

_____

_____

≈≈≈≈≈≈≈≈≈≈≈≈≈≈≈≈≈≈≈≈≈≈

# Making Requests

**Purpose: To practice making requests in different situations**

**What's Needed?**

→ 15 uninterrupted minutes

→ A quiet place to sit

→ A journal or pad of paper

→ A pencil or pen

**Instructions:**

1. In the following hypothetical scenario, assume that you are a parent speaking to your teenager.

**You say to your fourteen-year-old:**

*"When I see your dirty socks on the floor by the hamper, your pants draped over your dresser, and your shirt on the chair, I feel exasperated because this morning I understood you to say you'd pick up your dirty clothes before going to school."*

**Learning Questions:**

As the parent, what did you do to set your Intention?

_____

_____

_____

As the parent, what do you need?

_____

_____

What do you guess that your fourteen-year-old needs?

_____

_____

What will you say to your teenager to confirm that you've been understood?

_____

_____

_____

What will you say after your teenager tells you what she understood?

_____

_____

What will you say to her to invite her reaction?

_____

_____

What will you say after you hear the other person's reaction?

_____

_____

What request for action might you make to meet your need?

_____

_____

_____

How does your request take into consideration what your teenager might need?

_____

_____

_____

_____

2. In the following hypothetical situation, assume that you are a manager speaking to one of your employees.

   **You say to your employee:**
   _"When I read the report you wrote, I was troubled because I value teamwork and I need to be sure that we're on the same page."_

**Learning Questions:**

As the manager, what did you do to set your Intention?

_____

_____

As the manager, what do you need?

_____

What do you guess that your employee needs?

_____

_____

What will you say to your employee to confirm that you've been understood?

_____

_____

_____

What will you say after your employee tells you what he understood?

_____

_____

What will you say to him to invite his reaction?

_____

_____

What will you say after you hear his reaction?

_____

What request for action might you make to meet your need?

_____

_____

_____

How does your request take into consideration what your employee might need?

_____

_____

3. In the following hypothetical situation, assume that you are a teacher speaking to a student's parent.

   **You say:**
   "When I saw your son spit on the safety monitor,

*I felt shocked. I want to work with you to stop this behavior immediately."*

**Learning Questions:**

As the teacher, what did you do to set your Intention?

_____

_____

As the teacher, what do you need?

_____

What do you guess that the student's parent needs?

_____

_____

What will you say to the student's parent to confirm that you've been understood?

_____

_____

What will you say after the student's parent tells you what she understood?

_____

_____

What will you say to her to invite her reaction?

_____

_____

What will you say after you hear her reaction?

_____

What request for action might you make to meet your need?

_____

_____

_____

How does your request take into consideration what the student's parent might need?

_____

_____

_____

_____

# Conclusion

Conflict is a natural part of life, and probably always will be, as long as there are limited resources and people with different perspectives and opinions. Although most people feel uncomfortable with conflict, simply being involved in one is not the problem. The problem is how we deal with it.

Historically, human beings have employed two primary strategies for resolving conflicts: power-based and rights-based. With power-based strategies, the strongest or most powerful wins the argument, battle, or war, while rights-based strategies rely on rules and laws to determine who wins.

Recently, a strategy using interest-based negotiation has gained favor as a method for resolving conflicts. Interest-based approaches involve first listening to the feuding parties and then crafting agreements that address the disputants' key concerns as much as possible. Although this strategy leaves more people feeling satisfied than the winner-take-all approaches, it still falls short of creating deeper understanding or human connection.

Climbing divorce rates, religious community conflicts, road rage, public displays of fighting between members or spectators of professional and amateur sports teams, and the 9/11 destruction of lives and property demonstrate that people lack skills to live harmoniously and resolve conflicts peacefully. To do this, people need to learn to communicate in ways that bring common understanding with ease.

These skills are what Non-Adversarial Communication (NAC) is all about. As you practice them, you will begin to communicate in a way that deepens existing relationships, prevents conflicts, and deals more effectively with disagreements when they occur. You will find yourself with the skills to speak hard truths gracefully, and to treat others the way you wish to be treated.

Studying and practicing NAC awakens your emotional intelligence, improving your ability to identify your internal reactions to the life around you. As you begin to describe your reactions in terms of your human feelings and deep fundamental needs, you will gain clarity and a sense of personal responsibility that leads to successfully meeting your needs. In addition, because all human beings experience feelings and needs, NAC gives you a universal language that pairs the intellectual awareness of the head with the feeling intelligence of the heart to create understanding of yourself and others.

NAC conversations enable you to create understanding regardless of differences of opinion, perspective, culture, race, or gender. As a result, you will see others as more similar to yourself than different—as fellow human beings instead of enemies. When you choose to free your observations of the world from judgmental thoughts, and to express your feelings, needs, and requests in a non-threatening way, you will have conversations that connect you with others. That will lead to a world where everyone's needs are respected and valued, disagreements are worked through before they escalate, and conflicts are resolved peacefully.

# Guide to
# Daily Practice

*Practice is essential because . . . judging and blaming have become second nature to us. . . . We need to proceed slowly, think carefully before we speak, and often just take a deep breath and not speak at all. Learning the process and applying it both take time.*

*—Marshall Rosenberg*

## The Benefits of Daily Practice

Most people I know lead such busy lives that we rarely take even a few minutes to listen to ourselves in quiet, away from telephones, computers, televisions, and other people. One of the surprising benefits I discovered several years ago when I began taking five to fifteen minutes to sit quietly and reflect on my day was that I felt calmer, more relaxed, and more grounded.

Brain research over the past five years helps explain why it's so difficult to change behavior, even when we want to. Basically, when reading this book to learn new ways to respond using Non-Adversarial Communication, we are relaxed and receptive. But when we feel anger or other intense emotions, we cannot always act on new learnings and insights, because our rational brain can't intervene in time to short-circuit our hard-wired, automatic fight, flight, or freeze responses. At least not without practice.

According to psychotherapist and researcher Dr. Brent Atkinson, "one of the most enduring concepts in neuroscience is Hebb's Law, named after neuroscientist Donald Hebb, who stated that brain processes that occur together over and over again become grafted together, and are more likely to occur in conjunction in the future."

In other words, according to neurogenesis research, we can generate new neurons and neural pathways, creating new automatic responses if we rehearse over and over. In addition, I've found that a daily practice, much more so than sporadic practice, deepens our ability to remain in Intention (see pages 31–44), often long enough to avoid an adversarial reaction to what another says or does.

The best way to learn to listen deeply to others is to learn to listen to yourself. All the following activities provide an avenue to improve your ability to listen to yourself and to others, no matter their words or actions.

Participation in an ongoing practice group can complement and support your daily practice. Non-Adversarial Communication and Nonviolent Communication practice groups provide opportunities to use the skills with others, and to rehearse speaking and listening in preparation for real-life challenges.

We believe that it takes between twenty-one and thirty days of daily practice to deepen a new skill into a habit. For this reason, the following twelve activities are designed to encourage a short, daily practice for one month at a time. Daily practice takes commitment and is the key to success.

In order to get the most value from these activities, consider the few minutes to complete the activity as a gift that you give to yourself. Many find that scheduling a specific time of day to engage in the activity works best, because it creates a routine for yourself and others to honor. Create a comfortable space, a quiet environment, and freedom from interruption or distraction for the five to fifteen minutes it takes to engage in each exercise. Having a special notebook or journal will help you to keep your thoughts and reflections both private and organized. Choosing a special pen may enhance your enjoyment as well.

We recommend working sequentially through the following twelve activities, one per month. If you are highly motivated, you may wish to add one new activity per month and continue engaging in one or more of your earlier practices. No matter your preference, we recommend beginning with the Daily Check-in. (see Month 1 below).

If you make the investment of your time to engage in these practices, you will increase your emotional intelligence and shape your life to be less adversarial. You will:

→ Become more aware of how you personally experience life and how your internal reactions and your thoughts drive your behavior.

→ Become more conscious of your language and its impact on yourself and others.

→ Know how to change your communication to be more effective in dealing with yourself and with others.

# Deepening the Skills of Non-Adversarial Communication

## Month 1: Daily Check-in

Schedule a time to check in with yourself at least once each day. Set a consistent time, such as when you first wake up, while eating lunch, or before dinner, or commit to a time during the day by writing a time in your daily planner. Another way to do this is to set a daily reminder with an alarm on your computer. At the designated time, find a quiet place to sit uninterrupted for at least five minutes. Then ask yourself, "What am I feeling and needing right now?"

Be careful to answer with a pure feeling (none of those words that sound like feelings but are judgments in disguise) and a fundamental need. Feel free to get started by using the feelings lists on pages 91–92 and the needs list on page 110. (If you feel inclined, do this activity twice each day for stronger impact.)

## Month 2: Knowing Needs

We teach that approximately 80% of human connection is forged from identifying fundamental needs, and 20% from identifying feelings. Consciously identifying feelings enables us to understand our experience—our state of being—in the moment. But knowing feelings is not sufficient information to provide direction for making changes. It's important, therefore, to recognize that the greater contribution to understanding and to human connection comes from being able to identify needs.

Because it is essential in Non-Adversarial Communication to build a vocabulary of fundamental needs, we recommend the daily practice below.

**Week 1:** Use the Week 1 chart on the next page to learn the seven Needs Categories (shown in bold as Autonomy, Connection/Interdependence, Celebration, Integrity, Meaning, Peace, and Physical Well-Being), plus one word representing each need from the needs list (page 110).

It is important to select words that resonate with you. Their aim will be to remind you of the essence of the need on an experiential (in your body) level rather than merely on an intellectual level. Write one word in each column, as shown by the examples on the Week 1 chart.

**Week 2:** For each need, select one or two additional words from the needs list (page 110) that resonate with you and that will serve as other representative examples of the essence of the need for you. Write the one or two additional words in the appropriate columns on the Week 2 chart on page 177, as shown by the examples on that chart.

# Needs Categories
## Month 2: Knowing Needs - Week 1

| Autonomy | Connection/ Interdependence | Celebration | Integrity | Meaning | Peace | Physical Well-Being |
|----------|------------------------------|-------------|-----------|---------|-------|---------------------|
| Independence | Respect | Play | Authenticity | Clarity | Ease | Rest |
| | | | | | | |

# Needs Categories

## Month 2: Knowing Needs - Week 2

| Autonomy | Connection/ Interdependence | Celebration | Integrity | Meaning | Peace | Physical Well-Being |
|---|---|---|---|---|---|---|
| Independence Space Freedom | Respect Fairness Recognition | Play Joy Humor | Authenticity Self-worth Honesty | Clarity Purpose Effectiveness | Ease Order Beauty | Rest Movement Physical safety |

**Week 3:** At least once each day, observe what others say and do, and silently guess their fundamental human needs. You can do this during meetings, while watching television, while waiting in line at the market, during telephone conversations, when overhearing conversations in restaurants, etc.

**Week 4:** At least once each day, observe what another says and does, and risk guessing aloud the other's fundamental need.

## Month 3:  Create a Personal Joy List

Joy is both a need and a feeling. Many of us, myself included, need to consciously focus on what brings us joy in order to experience more of it in our lives. I found that a daily practice of adding to my Joy List stimulates and sensitizes my "joy sensors." Try it and see if it works for you!

Take a few moments each day to think of something you've seen, heard, or imagined that brings you joy or tickles you, pleases you, and/or elicits a smile from you when you remember it. Create your Personal Joy List by writing down one item each day for the next thirty days. Reread your entire list each day as you add to it. If you find that rereading the list lifts your spirits, feel free to add that to your list as well.

## Month 4:  Learn the Language of Feelings

Feelings are triggered by what we see, hear, or think.

Feelings are pointers to needs because the specific feelings that come alive are due to the underlying needs that are met or unmet by what we see, hear, or think. While not every environment supports the use of feeling words (for example, military or corporate environments), a feelings vocabulary is a key ingredient of emotional intelligence and, therefore, of Non-Adversarial Communication, whether you choose to verbally express and/ or guess feelings, or silently do so. For this reason, we offer a daily practice for expanding your vocabulary of feelings.

**You will need:**

→ 5–10 minutes per day for 30 days

→ Twelve 3 x 5 cards

→ A set of different-colored pencils, markers, or pens

→ A pencil or pen

**Instructions:**

1. Set-up: In a different color for each, respectively title the 3 x 5 cards one of the categories of feelings listed on the next page in bold. Then use a regular pen or pencil to write a list of three or four words commonly used to name feelings in each category, as shown in the examples on the next page. Select three or four words that resonate with you, and that you are therefore more likely to remember to use, from the feelings lists on pages 91–92.

**Glad:** Pleased, Thankful, Delighted, Elated

**Loving:** Nurtured, Moved, Tender

**Intrigued:** Curious, Fascinated, Surprised

**Hopeful:** Expectant, Encouraged, Optimistic

**Peaceful:** Calm, Relieved, Content, Secure

**Energetic:** Refreshed, Playful, Enthusiastic, Invigorated

**Mad:** Annoyed, Tense, Resentful, Aggravated

**Sad:** Disheartened, Dismayed, Hurt, Hopeless

**Scared:** Anxious, Apprehensive, Concerned, Terrified

**Confused:** Ambivalent, Bewildered, Torn, Overwhelmed

**Tired:** Fatigued, Weary, Exhausted

**Disconnected:** Alienated, Bored, Uninterested, Numb


**Weeks 1–3:** Spend five to ten minutes each day learning the Feelings Categories and the associated words on your twelve 3 x 5 cards.


**Week 4:** Repeat the daily practice of Weeks 1–3, plus the following: Sit quietly for three minutes each day this week. Ask yourself, "What am I feeling right now?" Write down all the feelings that you experience over the three minutes. Afterward, skim the feelings lists (pages 91–92) to verify that all the feelings you named are pure feelings rather than thoughts or judgments disguised as feelings. For each pure feeling, use the following format and fill in the blanks:

*"I feel _____ because I need _____."*

## Month 5: Cultivate an Attitude of Gratitude

Each day for the next thirty days, write down at least three things you heard or saw that day for which you feel grateful or appreciative.

In order to deepen your own experience of gratitude, as well as to increase the probability that another will receive your gratitude if you choose to express it, it is essential to identify the need that is met for you. To that end, it is important to use the formal Non-Adversarial Communication structure to write and/or state your observation, feeling, and need as follows:

*"When I hear you say (or see you do) _____, I feel grateful (or appreciative) because that met my need for _____."*

Of the three statements of gratitude, include at least one for yourself, using the same format.

## Month 6: Become Proficient with Phrasing

Each day for the next thirty days, be conscious of your use of words and phrasing.

**Week 1:** Pay attention to your use of the word "feelings." Typically we are expressing our thoughts rather than our feelings when we follow "I feel" with "that," "like," "as if," or "you." Each time you catch yourself saying "I feel that...," or "I feel like...," or "I feel as if...," or "I feel you...," restate it so that you follow "I feel" with a feeling from the lists on pages 91–92.

**Week 2:** Each day, repeat the daily activities of Week 1. This week, each time you become aware of saying "I feel" followed by a thought, restate your thought into your feeling and need ("I feel _____ because I need _____.")

**Weeks 3–4:** Repeat the daily activities of Weeks 1 and 2. In addition, when you hear yourself say "I have to," "I should," "I ought to," or "I must," restate it into "I feel _____ because I need _____, so I choose to _____," or "I feel _____ because I need _____, and I want to _____," or "I feel _____ because I need _____ and I would like to _____."

## Month 7: Focus on What You Want, Not on What You Don't Want

When we want something to happen or someone, including our self, to do something, we are focusing on a strategy that we consciously or unconsciously believe will meet our needs. Because many of us are more aware of what we don't want than what we do want, we recommend this daily practice for rephrasing your requests into ones that will more successfully meet your needs.

For one month, notice each day whether you focus on what you don't want or on what you do want. Each time you hear yourself state what you don't want, stop and take a moment to identify the need you want to meet. Then use positive language to restate your need and the request that you hope will meet your need.

**For example:**

*"I would like _____, and I wonder if you would be willing to _____," or "I would like you to _____ because that will meet my need for _____."*

As you describe what you do want, be sure that your request is do-able and specific, and that your timeline is clear. Finally, ask if the other person would be willing to let you know what she understands to be your request and the need you hope will be met.

## Month 8: Find a New Perspective

This daily activity is based on Rachel Naomi Remen's book, *My Grandfather's Blessings,* and is a way to teach our self to look at our life in new ways.

Each day for the next thirty days, think about the day you've just lived. Take ten to fifteen minutes to write down your responses to these three questions:

→ Today, what surprised you?

→ Today, what moved or touched you?

→ Today, what inspired you?

As you reflect on what you observed that evoked feelings of surprise, of being moved, or of inspiration, write down what need was met or unmet by each of the three experiences.

Over the course of the month, notice whether your awareness of feeling surprised, moved, or inspired begins to occur closer in time to when you actually experienced these feelings.

## Month 9: Shift from "Have to" to "Want to"

**Week 1:** Keep a daily log with two columns. In the left column, record one thing you did each day because you "had to." Leave the column on the right blank. At the end of Week 1, use the needs list (page 110) to identify and write in the right column the need you were meeting by doing each item listed in the left column.

**Week 2:** Repeat Week 1, but each night fill in the right column with the need you were meeting by engaging in the action listed in the left column.

**Weeks 3 and 4:** Each time you say to yourself or think, "I'm doing _____ because I have to," restate it into "I'm doing _____ because that will meet my need for _____." Notice if your energy shifts from resisting the behavior to welcoming the behavior.

## Month 10: Meeting Your Needs

For the next month, sit quietly each day for five minutes, asking yourself, "What do I feel and need right now?" If helpful, use the needs list (page 110). After five minutes, write down the need that's most strongly resonating internally for you, or more strongly than the others.

Then think of three strategies (requests) to meet those needs, at least one of which you can do for yourself without involving others.

## Month 11:  Change Demands into Requests

This month, pay attention to the words you use when wanting another person to do something. Ask yourself, "How will I react if this person says 'no'?" "Am I making a request or am I making a demand?"

If you realize that you would be angry if the person said "no," or you hear yourself saying or thinking "You must...," or "You have to...," or "You should...," or "You're supposed to...," then take time before engaging with the other person.

Instead of rushing to interact, first silently ask yourself, "What is my Intention? Is it to create a connection with this person so that each of us feels the other understands what's important, or is my Intention to persuade, coerce, or force the other to do what I want?"

If you want to create understanding, then silently identify what you see and hear, and what need is unmet for you. Once you know what need of yours is unmet, ask yourself what the other person might need.

Finally, practice changing your words to "I need _____ and I'm guessing you need _____, is that accurate?" After you are clear about what the other person needs, restate your request so that it addresses both your need and the other person's need.

## Month 12:  Change a Habit

**Week 1:** Take five minutes each day this week to ask yourself, "What habit or belief would I like to change because it no longer serves me? What needs am I meeting by continuing this habit or belief? What needs would I meet by changing this habit or belief?" By the end of Week 1, select one habit or belief to focus on for the remainder of the month.

**Weeks 2–3:** Develop a daily practice to remind yourself to watch out for this habit or belief. Each time you think of the habit or belief that no longer serves you, think about what needs you will meet by changing your behavior or belief. Some strategies to increase your conscious awareness of this habit or belief follow.

→ Wear a specific bracelet or a rubber band on your wrist. Each time you look at it (several times each day), remind yourself to watch out for the habit or belief that no longer serves you. For one minute, imagine yourself behaving or believing as you desire yourself to be, and state what need(s) you will be meeting by behaving or believing in this new way.

→ Write a brief description on a 3 x 5 card of how you want to behave or believe. Post the card in your car, on your computer, on your bathroom mirror—

someplace you will see it several times each day. Each time you look at it, remind yourself to watch out for the habit or belief that no longer serves you. For one minute, imagine yourself behaving or believing as you desire yourself to be, and state what need(s) you will be meeting by behaving or believing in this new way.

→ Set an alarm on your computer calendar that pops up when you aren't expecting it. Each time the alarm goes off, remind yourself to watch out for the habit or belief that no longer serves you. For one minute, imagine yourself behaving or believing as you desire yourself to be, and state what need(s) you will be meeting by behaving or believing in this new way.

→ Identify something you do at least once each day (e.g., wash your hands, open your US postal mail, answer your telephone, walk through a specific door- way, place the key in your car ignition). Each time you engage in the specific activity, take one minute to imagine yourself already being the person you wish to be, someone who behaves or believes as you desire.

**Week 4:** Continue the daily practices of Weeks 2–3, plus each time you realize that you acted out of your old habit or belief with another, risk going back and undoing the old way of behaving or believing, as shown below, for example:

**If another person is involved, use NAC to express yourself as follows:**

*"When I realize that I did (or said) _____, I feel _____, because my response didn't meet my need for _____, and I'm guessing you need _____. I'm wondering if you would be comfortable if I change my response to how I wish I had responded?"*

**After you respond in your desired way, check in with yourself several times over the next twenty-four hours by asking yourself:**

*"When I think of how I changed my response, how do I feel? What do I need?"*

# Suggested Reading

Atkinson, Brent J. "Altered States: Why Insight Itself Isn't Enough for Lasting Change." *Psychotherapy Networker*, September/October 2004. www.thecouplesclinic.com/ Altered_States.htm (accessed September 12, 2006).

Bennett-Goleman, Tara. *Emotional Alchemy: How the Mind Can Heal the Heart*. New York: Three Rivers Press, 2001.

Childre, Doc, and Howard Martin (with Donna Beech). *The HeartMath Solution*. New York: HarperCollins Publishers, 1999.

Dass, Ram, and Paul Gorman. *How Can I Help? Stories and Reflections on Service*. New York: Alfred A. Knopf, 1985.

Fisher, Roger, and William Ury (with Bruce Patton, ed.). *Getting to Yes: Negotiating Agreement Without Giving In*. 2nd ed. New York: Penguin Books, 1991.

Hughes, Marcia, L. Bonita Patterson, and James Bradford Terrell. *Emotional Intelligence In Action: Training and Coaching Activities for Leaders and Managers*. San Francisco: Pfeiffer, 2005.

Leu, Lucy. *Nonviolent Communication Companion Workbook: A Practical Guide for Individual, Group, or Classroom Study*. Encinitas, CA: PuddleDancer Press, 2003.

Maslow, Abraham H. *Motivation and Personality*. 2nd ed. New York: Harper & Row, 1970.

Maslow, Abraham H. *Toward a Psychology of Being.* New York: Van Nostrand Reinhold Company, 1968.

Mayer, John, and Peter Salovey. "Emotional Intelligence and the Construction and Regulation of Feelings." *Applied and Preventive Psychology* 4, no. 3 (1995): 197–208.

Pinker, Steven. *How the Mind Works.* New York: W. W. Norton & Company, 1997.

Remen, Rachel Naomi. *My Grandfather's Blessings: Stories of Strength, Refuge, and Belonging.* New York: Riverhead Books, 2000.

Rosenberg, Marshall B. *Nonviolent Communication: A Language of Life.* Encinitas, CA: PuddleDancer Press, 2003.

Tolle, Eckhart. *The Power of Now.* Novato, CA: New Word Library and Namaste Publishing, 1999.

Weisinger, Hendrie. *Emotional Intelligence at Work.* San Francisco: Jossey-Bass, Inc., 1998.

# About the Authors

# About the Authors

**Arlene Brownell** and **Thomas Bache-Wiig** cofounded *Connection Partners, Inc.*, a mediation, facilitation, and training company, in 1999. Together and independently, they strive to be catalysts for clarity, understanding, and human connection.

**Arlene Brownell**'s professional career spans over 30 years and includes her contributions as an interdisciplinary social scientist, manager, organizational consultant, and executive coach for senior federal employees. She holds a BA in Psychology and an MA in Community and Clinical Psychology from California State University, Long Beach, and a PhD in Social Ecology from the University of California, Irvine. Following her PhD, she completed a two-year postdoctoral research fellowship in Public Health at UCLA. Arlene has also completed several advanced trainings with The Center for Nonviolent Communication.

As a mediator, collaborative divorce coach, group facilitator, and Non-Adversarial Communication trainer, Arlene works with individuals, couples, families, neighbors, organizations, and faith communities.

Arlene has published over 80 articles in professional and lay periodicals on diverse topics, such as adult learning; stress, coping, and chronic illness; aligning values and performance; preventing sexual harassment; economic change, life events, and depression; training measurement and evaluation; Non-Adversarial Communication skills to enhance collaboration; and the benefits of mediation to business.

Arlene loves to hike, snowshoe, and ride her tandem bike with her husband, Tom Bache-Wiig.

**Thomas Bache-Wiig** worked with more than 400 businesses in his previous career as an independent sales representative, bringing to successful resolution countless negotiations and conflicts. His business experience enhances his work as a mediator, collaborative divorce coach, group facilitator, Non-Adversarial Communication trainer, and Visiting Program Manager for the federal government's Conflict Resolution Skills course.

In addition to earning his BS in Business from Regis University, Tom has completed extensive training with The Center for Nonviolent Communication, and has had over 25 years of experience resolving business and relationship disputes. He strives for balance between the practical and the ideal, and between risks and benefits, whether he is designing or facilitating group processes, or helping others to reach solutions. With expertise in Interest-Based Negotiation, process facilitation, and Non-Adversarial Communication, Tom seeks to find themes, reframe concerns, structure conversation, pace meetings, identify needs, and ask the right questions at the right time.

Tom has a passion for skiing, running, cycling, hiking, and for Arlene Brownell, his wife of over 28 years.

For more information about the authors, their trainings, and other conflict resolution services, please go to:

**www.connectionpartners.com**

# To Contact Us:

## Write to:

Connection Partners, Inc.
P.O. Box 2513
Lyons, CO 80540


## or visit our website at:

www.connectionpartners.com

Printed in the United States
71503LV00004B/28